KILLER
COUPLES

KILLER
COUPLES

Ten Couples Who
Killed Together

JONNY CASSIDY

Contents

Introduction

When two people come together in life, whether wedded or not, they can accomplish great things. It's wonderful to have friends, but sometimes it's only that special someone with whom we share an intimate connection who can truly understand us and be a partner in the true sense of the word. This special and powerful human relationship is typically used to build a family and a life together. People in love can use their bond to work as a team toward a variety of other positive goals, whether they are professional pursuits, diverse adventures, or anything else.

However, like most things involving human beings, a couple's love can lead down some extremely dark paths. These dark paths are most usually manifested as fighting, domestic abuse, or any number of other challenges that plague relationships, but they can also be a partnership in crime on rare occasions. Many couples have embarked on a journey to crime throughout history, but not all of them have the potential to leave a romantic trail in popular culture and be remembered in the same manner that Bonnie and Clyde were. There is no other way to describe some couples and their deeds except as pure evil in some circumstances.

The couples who decide to kill together, especially for the mere pleasure of it, are certainly a rare phenomenon. These matches made in hell can come together under an array of different, unique circumstances in their lives. As with other killers, particularly serial ones, there's virtually always a history that can explain much of what has happened or at least provide hints as to how these people ended up the way they are.

In a strange and dark twist, the intimate understanding and compassion that come with a romantic relationship often wind up encouraging the worst in these individuals. In many of these cases, suppressed demons, dark urges, and morbid, violent fantasies that would otherwise remain repressed might surface and manifest in the real world. These murderous couples will fuel each other's evil impulses, but healthy, regular individuals in love will feed each other's goodness and bring out the best in each other.

In other cases, it's not so much that two killers have discovered the murderous urges in each other as it is that there is manipulation at play. Unfortunately, even the best of human qualities such as love can be abused, and even a perfectly normal individual can find themselves being dragged down into the abyss because of blind love. This book will take a look at ten cases where two people had joined forces to do the unthinkable. These murderers come from a range of different backgrounds, and, like the tales of other serial killers, their disturbing stories provide insight into the many ways in which people can go down a path of carnage. Even though it can be difficult to fully understand the deranged minds of these people, their stories are sure to put the problems of regular people's relationships into a whole new perspective.

CHAPTER ONE

Frederick and Rosemary West

Childhood trauma, rape, incest, and murder were only some of the grizzly elements of this infamous couple's murderous story. The Wests have permanently ingrained themselves into Britain's history as some of the most deranged people to ever be caught committing a crime. The torture and the killings that Fred and Rose committed between 1967 and 1987 would leave a lasting scar and traumatize the city of Gloucester in the English county of Gloucestershire forever.

The background stories of these two killers, which were very disturbing in their own right, were a significant aspect of this case. Fred and Rose were textbook examples of people who were on a dark path from the start. Given their similarly horrific backgrounds, one has to question whether these two were somehow drawn to each other before they met and married. Only a small percentage of people will experience what Rose and Fred did, and even fewer will find someone so similar to them. The fact that the West's own children were also harmed by them added to the shock. Like other serial killers, they tortured and murdered strangers, but the horrifying events that occurred in their own home brought the case to a whole other level of disturbing.

Fred and Rose's Backgrounds

Fred's parents, Walter Stephen West and Daisy Hannah Hill were impoverished farmers in a village called Much Marcle, which is located in the Herefordshire county of England. Fred was born Frederick Walter Stephen West on September 29, 1941, at Bickerton Cottage, and he was the second child born to Daisy. He was the first child to survive, though, as one of his brothers died in the first few months after birth. In total, Daisy gave birth to eight children, two of whom passed away in infancy. The family was close, and they mostly kept to themselves.

As the police later learned, mostly from the extensive interviews conducted with Fred after his arrest, his home environment while he was growing up was allegedly bizarre, incestuous, and deeply scarring for him and his siblings. Many of Fred's claims were contradicted by the testimony of his brother Doug, who said that Fred made up the stories of molestation and incest, so the full extent of abuse and molestation at the farm is unclear.

As Fred alleged, his father had incestuous relationships with his sisters, and incest was commonplace in their household. Furthermore, Fred claimed that his father urged him to have childhood encounters with bestiality. Walter taught Fred that he could do whatever he wanted as long as he didn't get caught, and this was a lesson he had learned since he was a child. Walter, on the other hand, insisted on strict adherence to the few regulations that did exist in the home. This discipline was mostly based on the children's responsibilities, which included numerous chores, seasonal work, and a variety of tasks around the farmstead.

Fred's mother was not exempt from shocking allegations, and he claims that she has raped and assaulted him since he was a teenager. His mother, he subsequently revealed, was the one who first introduced him to sex when he was just twelve years old. She was fiercely protective of her children, to the point of being overprotective. This was particularly true about Fred, who was undoubtedly his mother's favorite child and would later be regarded by many of his peers as a mama's boy. Fred didn't make his allegations out of hatred or anger, though. He simply stated them as facts of his story, but the truth is that he was very attached to his mother while growing up.

Walter and Daisy moved a few times while they were still raising their children, eventually settling at Moorcourt Farm in 1946. The family remained impoverished throughout Fred's childhood, living without electricity, running water, or a bathroom. Fred knew what it was like to have to work for a living from the time he was a child. Fred developed a work ethic as a result of these experiences, but his persistent lack of basic needs, much alone comforts, taught him that thievery was an option at times. Fred developed a liking for petty theft once he started doing it, and he kept it for the rest of his life.

All the while, Fred was going to school in the hope of getting a valuable education. Fred displayed certain artistic tendencies and even some skills in specific crafts, such as woodworking, while he was in school. In terms of his education, he struggled with much of the curriculum and was a slow learner. During the subsequent trial proceedings, Fred's former classmates described him as a somewhat

dim child who was prone to lethargy, disinterest, and troublesome behavior. Fred never fully mastered writing or reading, and he remained semi-illiterate well into adulthood.

Due to his poor academic performance, Fred eventually gave up on school and left in late 1956 when he was just fifteen. He had work waiting for him back at Moorcourt Farm, so he immediately started as a laborer after dropping out of school. He spent the next two years in this way until he got into a near-fatal motorcycle accident in 1958, which left him with broken limbs and a skull fracture. The fracture resulted in an eight-day coma and possibly had ramifications for his behavior from that point on. Notably, other family members noticed that he was more prone to uncontrolled outbursts of anger. Fred hurt his head yet again two years after this accident when he fell from a fire staircase. The fall, however, happened when he was pushed by a girl whom he tried to grope.

Fred's good looks drew the attention of young girls, and he was able to attract quite a bit of attention from the opposite sex in his youth. The problem was that as soon as the females got close to Fred, they discovered that he had an unstable, aggressive personality. He was obnoxious and aggressive, frequently grabbing ladies and harassing them as he pleased. When he was first arrested for molesting a 13-year-old girl, he was just twenty years old. The girl he molested was his younger sister, Kitty, who told their mother that Fred had been sexually assaulting her for a while, even saying that he got her pregnant. He was able to evade serious legal repercussions, mostly because Kitty didn't want to testify, but the incident left a lasting mark on his relationship with his family, and he was forced to leave home. He stayed in Much Marcle, but he moved to a house owned by his aunt. Fred would re-establish contact with his parents in 1962, but he remained largely cut-off.

Rose Letts, Fred's eventual second wife and partner in crime, was born Rosemary Pauline Letts on November 29, 1953, in Northam, Devon, England. William Andrew Letts and Daisy Gwendoline Fuller were her parents. Rose's family was also large, just like Fred's, and she was the fifth of seven children, also born into an impoverished family. Rose's mother, who had problems with severe depression, was undergoing therapy while still carrying Rose. The doctors saw fit to subject her to electroconvulsive therapy, which was probably what contributed to the many difficulties that Daisy experienced during this particular pregnancy and might have caused injuries to unborn Rose.

Growing up, Rose had similar experiences and issues as Fred. Already in her teenage years, Rose was prone to anger and mood swings while also performing badly in her studies. Unlike Fred, though, Rose had the experience of divorce as her parents separated while she was still a teen. After the separation, Rose spent a few months with her mom before moving to her father's home in Bishop's Cleeve, Gloucestershire, when she was sixteen.

Unfortunately, Rose's father had even worse mental problems than her mother, suffering from schizophrenia and a very violent temper. Rose, just like her sister

Patricia, had to endure both physical abuse and sexual molestation. Unsurprisingly, Rose began to develop peculiar ideas and attitudes toward her sexuality as she grew. She acquired a strange fascination with her own body, often walking naked around the house, purposely in front of her younger brothers, Graham and Gordon. When she was only thirteen, Rose began to molest her young brothers at night.

Marriage and Increased Violence

Fred's first marriage wasn't to Rose, but a girl called Catherine Costello, nicknamed Rena. At the time when they got on a path to marriage in September of 1962, Fred was 21 and had just reentered a relationship with her after a prolonged hiatus. In the time that they spent apart leading up to this marriage, Rena worked as a prostitute in Scotland's city of Glasgow. She also came back pregnant, but their shared history and Rena's tolerance of Fred's crude behavior toward women made him rekindle the relationship. The two got married just two months later, in November of 1962, after which they relocated to Coatbridge, Lanarkshire.

Rena gave birth to a daughter, whom they named Charmaine Carol, in February of 1963. In July of 1964, the couple had their own child, another daughter named Anne Marie. As they were raising the family, Fred sought work and eventually settled for the job of an ice cream driver. According to witnesses such as the family's babysitter, Isa McNeil, Rena was a committed mother who did her best with her daughters. Fred, on the other hand, was a strict father who would keep his children locked up in their lower bunk beds and only let them out when he was at work. Rena's parents had disapproved of her first, mixed-race child, so the couple had moved to Glasgow by the time they had Anna Marie. Around this time, Fred and his family met Anne McFall, a 16-year-old girl, through their babysitter. The girl became friends with the Wests and spent a lot of time in their apartment, dealing with her boyfriend's recent tragic death at work.

The marriage was already in crisis at this point, not just because of Fred's violent tendencies but also his numerous affairs, one of which resulted in a pregnancy. Rena soon caught wind of Fred's indiscretions, and she responded in kind, beginning an affair with one John McLachlan. McLachlan was an important witness years later, having quite a few things to say about Fred West's behavior and attitudes. He described him as a sadist who particularly enjoyed beating and tormenting women and young children while being quick to surrender when confronted by men. McLachlan would often beat Fred in response to his domestic abuse of Rena. On one occasion, McLachlan was present when Fred hit young Charmaine over the head simply because she asked for some ice cream, which led to another beating by McLachlan.

Things took a severely dark turn in November of 1965 when Fred was involved in a traffic accident in which he ran over a small boy with his ice cream van. A police investigation determined that it was an accident, and Fred wasn't charged with anything. However, the tragedy created quite an upset in the local Glasgow community, and Fred was fearful of retribution, so the Wests, along with Isa McNeil and Anne McFall, moved to Bishop's Cleeve Gloucestershire. They rented a caravan there, and all lived in it together.

Fred's sadistic inclinations and violent attitudes toward women reached a new high during this period. He was sexually sadistic toward his wife, abusive toward the other women in the house, and more aggressive with the children, particularly Charmaine, his stepdaughter. He even persuaded his own wife to return to prostitution to supplement the family's income. Anne McFall, on the other hand, had gotten attached to Fred and had been by his side throughout his journey. Anne's support was notably evident when Rena conspired with McLachlan to help her, McNeil, and the kids escape from Fred. Anne informed Fred about the plan as soon as she learned about it. Rena and McNeil were finally able to flee due to the involvement of McLachlan and the police, but unfortunately, Rena's daughters stayed with Fred. She would frequently visit her daughters, but in her absence, Anne McFall gradually assumed a motherly role.

Anne eventually began trying to talk Fred into divorcing Rena and marrying her, but this never came to fruition. In July of 1967, Anne disappeared at the age of eighteen. She was in her eighth month of pregnancy, carrying Fred's child. Her disappearance was never reported to the police, and she didn't turn up again until the remnants of her mutilated body were discovered near Much Marcle in June 1994. The police concluded that her hands were tied before she was murdered and that the killer may have even cut her unborn baby out of her womb, based on the evidence they obtained. This contradicted Fred's account, in which he stated after his arrest that he stabbed her during an altercation.

Rosemary Letts and the Murderous Culmination

The hellish match was made when Fred met Rose Letts while still technically married to Rena in late November of 1968. Fred was now 27, while Rose was only 15, having her birthday on the day they met. Rose moved in with Fred in his caravan by her following birthday, but they soon moved to a house on Midland Road in Gloucester. It wasn't long until Rose got pregnant by Fred, and the two had a daughter, Heather Anne, born in October 1970. Fred's old thieving habits got him in trouble less than two months later, and things went from bad to worse. He was apprehended and imprisoned until the summer of 1971.

In his absence, Rose was left to care for their daughter and Fred's other two children. As the police later determined, Rose most likely murdered Charmaine during Fred's imprisonment. As it turned out, Rose was just as sadistic as Fred and was terribly abusive to the girls. Anne Marie testified that Rose beat her and Charmaine all the time, taking pleasure in the crying of her victims. According to Anne Marie, Charmaine purposely refused to cry, which brought on additional scorn and contempt from Rose, resulting in severe beatings. After Fred returned in late June to find that his stepdaughter had disappeared, Rose told him that Rena had come and taken her home. Of course, this was a lie, and Rena came to visit in August of that year with the intention of taking her daughter away, but she, too, vanished soon after.

Fred and Rose married in late January of 1972 in Gloucester, and already on June 1, the newlyweds had another daughter, named Mae. Fred soon began to pressure his current wife, just like his first, to go into prostitution. Things around the home continued to escalate further into derangement, especially sexually. In total, Rose would have seven children, of which at least three were undoubtedly extramarital since they were mixed-race. When the family moved to a new, bigger home on Cromwell Street, Fred designated and redesigned a special room for Rose's prostitution work. The room was called "Rose's Room," and it was to be used strictly for her customers. Fred created holes in the wall through which he could watch what was happening. The children knew not to enter the room or come close when Rose was with a customer by looking at the red light that was set up next to the door. In one of the most bizarre twists of all, Rose's own biological father was a frequent customer.

In October of 1972, the couple tried to involve their 17-year-old nanny, Caroline Roberts, in their extreme sexual activities, which scared her away from the job. Nonetheless, they managed to lure her back in December, after which they raped her together. The incident was reported to the police, but when it came time for the trial, Caroline was terrified to testify, and the case fell apart. The Wests only had to pay a 50-pound fine. This was the definitive beginning of the Wests' series of rapes and eventual murders.

Anne Marie, who was just eight years old when she was first raped in early 1973, was their next victim. After keeping her chained in the cellar, it was largely Fred who assaulted her, while Rosemary stood by and watched. Years later, Anne Marie became pregnant but had a miscarriage, prompting her to flee her home in 1979. In her absence, Heather Anne became the primary target of the couple's brutality before disappearing sometime later.

The Wests had spent the entire decade of the 1970s, unbeknownst to the rest of the world, raping, torturing, and murdering women and girls from all sorts of backgrounds. The shocking revelations began in 1992, when Fred began filming his misdeeds, beginning in May of that year with the rape of another of his daughters, Louise. Louise sought help from her mother after being sodomized, brutalized, and nearly strangled, and was told by Rose that she was asking for it. Both parents continued to molest Louise from that point on until she finally garnered the strength to tell a friend at school, after which the information got to the police.

In august of 1992, both Fred and Rosemary were charged with rape and child cruelty, after which their children were taken away and put into foster care. The prosecution for rape soon hit a dead end due to a lack of witness cooperation, but this time, the police persevered. They continued to investigate the family, particularly the disappearance of Heather. Based on tips and testimonies from children, the investigators soon acquired a search warrant for the Wests' home, after which all the horror soon began coming to light. Searches and excavations began in February of 1994, and the police uncovered human remains all over the yard. Fred originally confessed to Heather's murder, but after some time had passed, he admitted to at least nine other murders. Rosemary was soon arrested and charged.

Fred was charged with 11 murders, while Rose was charged with 10, however, at least two more were likely committed. The majority of these killings occurred between 1971 and 1979, with the addition of Heather Anne West's murder in June 1987. Fred evaded justice by hanging himself in his cell in Birmingham in 1995, but Rosemary was sentenced to life without the possibility of parole, which is a sentence she is serving to this day at age 67. The West family home and property were razed to the ground.

CHAPTER TWO

Susan and James Carson

How two murderers in a relationship feed each other's urges and deranged fantasies sometimes go far enough to be described as something called *shared psychotic disorder*, also known as folie á deux in the case of couples. This phenomenon can manifest in two or more people at a time, and it's characterized by a deep emotional connection between people who begin to share in all sorts of delusions. Cults are a common example of places where this rare type of psychosis can occur, illustrated by incidents where groups of people get so caught up in a delusional narrative or fantasy that they begin externalizing that fantasy collectively and very destructively such as by violent action against others or mass suicide.

In couples or groups of people with shared psychotic disorder, there is usually an instigator, referred to as the active partner, while the other person embraces the instigator's delusions and gradually becomes locked into this twisted world. This person is known as the passive partner in shared psychotic disorder. A textbook example of this disorder was a murderous California couple in the 1980s, consisting of Susan Barnes Carson and James Clifford Carson. Referring to themselves as vegetarian Muslim warriors, the two lovers went on to kill people whom they believed to be witches.

Background and the Path to Insanity

The descent into madness for these two people had started well before they met and fell in love, even though many aspects of their background stories are surprisingly normal. James Clifford Carson or Michael Bear Carson, which he later went by, was born on November 28 of 1941 in Oklahoma. In the mid-1970s, just a few years before the killings began in 1981, "Michael" was still James, a relatively normal family man. He had a master's degree in Chinese studies from the University of Iowa and a range of different interests, including history, theology, and philosophy. Before graduating, Michael had already gotten married, and just after he graduated from the university, he and his wife had a daughter named Jennifer, and they moved to Arizona.

According to the later testimonies by his daughter, he paid enough attention to her and the family and was a good father, at least early on. His marital arrangement gradually became somewhat unconventional, though, but not in an overly negative manner. Namely, there was a period when his wife was the primary breadwinner, leaving him as a stay-at-home dad. On the side, Michael made some income by selling marijuana. This arrangement wasn't a source of much friction at home, but James' behavior did gradually begin to shift. More and more, his rebellious, non-conformist nature began to take hold, and the regularity of middle-class life perhaps became a source of personal frustration.

Michael became an angrier man than he was before, more withdrawn, overall unstable, and seemingly uninterested in the family life he had begun. He also refused to look for work and change his increasingly destructive lifestyle. His wife tolerated this for a while, but as things escalated, the marriage started to fall apart. In 1977, James' wife had had enough, and she took Jennifer with her, moved away, and filed for divorce. It wasn't long until soon-to-be Michael met Susan.

Susan Barnes Carson was older than Michael; she was born on September 14, 1941. Nonetheless, her first life shared many parallels with Michael's. She, too, lived a suburban, upper-middle-class existence as a seemingly accomplished and successful housewife with two teenage sons in Scottsdale, Arizona, in the 1960s. Susan's husband was a successful man who more than provided for the family, and neither she nor her children ever lacked anything. Susan, however, was fundamentally unhappy, and a feeling that she was missing out on life was a heavy weight on her mind.

Susan turned to drugs, particularly the psychedelics that were becoming prevalent at the time, such as LSD, peyote, mescaline, and other hallucinogens to escape her unfulfilling existence. Susan's abnormal behavior became even worse when she began to welcome the attention of her sons' teenage friends and classmates. She began seducing and sleeping with them soon after.

Susan's drug habit and its profound effects were further fueled by her long-standing idea that she had psychic abilities. Susan began to regularly hallucinate at the age of 35, sober or not, as a result of her severe drug use and her delusions. She referred to her hallucinations as visions, fueling her downward spiral even more. Her behavior deteriorated into psychosis, and she grew fascinated with the idea of transforming into a "new" version of herself. Susan's marriage was in shambles at this point, of course, and it eventually fell apart.

This personal reinvention that she had begun was what led her to start calling herself "Suzan" instead of "Susan." In her "visions," Suzan fantasized about meeting her soulmate and new lifelong partner. This was when Suzan first met James, and the two soul-searching divorcees immediately formed a strong connection. The fateful encounter happened in 1978 at a party where the two ran into each other by chance.

As James' daughter later testified, it was at this point that her father's descent into madness reached a point of no return, owing to the influence that Suzan had on him right from the start. In an interview she gave in recent years, Jennifer explained how her father was the sort of person who read stories to his daughter and braided her hair, but after meeting Suzan, this man was gone. Jennifer, just like her mom, was aware that something had been wrong with her father for quite a while, but she believed that Suzan was the final straw and, from then on, James would barely even look at his family. It was ultimately Suzan who "renamed" James to Michael, using Biblical inspiration. Due to this and other influences she had on Michael, it's safe to assume that Suzan was the mastermind behind the murders.

After Suzan and Michael Bear were firmly on their path to a drug-fueled rebirth, Michael wrote a letter to Jennifer, telling her of his new path and how it was God who reinvented him as "Michael." Suzan regarded Michael as some kind of disciple, which was precisely what she had been looking for based on her hallucinations. Michael had always had a profound interest in theology, spirituality, and the search for God, and this was possibly one of the key reasons why they attracted each other so quickly. Michael and Suzan were, in Jennifer's words, "like two magnets that immediately flew to each other."

The Final Descent and the
Beginning of the Witch Hunt

After the separation and divorce between her parents, Jennifer would still spend some weekends at her father's new place, which was Suzan's townhouse in Scottsdale. Jennifer spoke of these weekends as if they were a horror film, describing the couple's home as a haunted forest instead of adorning the home with many small trees kept in pots. She explained how they had almost no furniture and very little illumination. Jennifer would have to sleep on the floor in a sleeping bag whenever she came over, and the Bears would hardly feed her. Unsurprisingly, Suzan was also abusive, both physically and verbally, and the house was full of drugs. Suzan and Michael would often just lie in bed all day, naked, sleeping the day away after a nightlong drug bender.

Suzan and Michael eventually sold the townhouse and would use much of the money to fund a sort of spiritual trip across the world, including locales like Israel, India, the UK, and France. They got officially married in 1978 during this trip, engaging in an unorthodox, nocturnal ceremony under a full moon at the famous Stonehenge in England. Suzan used time and inspiration while visiting Europe to further consolidate her ideology and her distinct approach to religion. Suzan and Michael adopted Islam and put a different spin on it using hard drugs, hallucinogens, and psychosis as fuel.

Needless to say, the interpretation was radical. They also tried to preach this new religion to the world while traveling, but they were wholly unsuccessful. The two started to consider themselves vegetarian Muslim warriors, with one of their more extreme beliefs being that anyone who insults a woman should be put to death. Suzan's hallucination, in which she was told that the couple should adopt Islam, also told her that they should kill "witches." One of the primary aspects of this "religion" was the belief in the existence of witches and their presence everywhere. Suzan believed that these witches were psychics like her and that they were using their telepathic powers to control others.

The newlyweds returned to San Francisco after they ran out of money, and they initially stayed in a motel. While going on one of their LSD trips in this motel, Suzan had another vision, this time revolving even more around concrete action. Suzan told Michael that she saw the vision of a prophet who gave her a list of witches in this world whom they were supposed to kill, which was God's will. Some of the individuals on this list were rather famous, such as Ronald Reagan and the then-Governor of California, Jerry Brown. Suzan dictated the list from her vision as Michael wrote it down, and they devised an actual plan to assassinate the POTUS. A hiker passing through an area where the

Bears were camped eventually discovered the written details of the plot and notified the police. The threat was taken seriously enough by the authorities that Jennifer and her mother were visited by the Secret Service in 1982.

Not long after returning to the US, Suzan and Michael moved in with one Keryn Barnes, a 23-year-old girl living in San Francisco's Haight-Ashbury district. Keryn was a young girl with dreams of making it big in California and becoming a star while also having an interest in spiritual pursuits. Along the way, she was drawn in by the hippie community in Haight-Ashbury, by that point a well-known hotspot of drugs and hippie living. The couple met Keryn at a party in 1980, and her interest in spirituality was complemented by the Bear couple's search for new members of their would-be cult. Keryn's fascination with the things that Suzan and Michael preached was quite refreshing for them, as most had shunned their weird behavior and beliefs up to that point.

The Bear couple and Keryn continued to use a lot of drugs, especially LSD, throughout their lives together. Things took a problematic turn when Keryn refused to enter into a romantic relationship with the couple, who wanted her to become Michael's second wife of sorts. After these disagreements, Suzan began having visions in which she saw that Keryn was a witch who was trying to steal her psychic and yogic powers. Not long after that, Suzan told her husband and disciple to kill the witch.

Michael attacked Keryn in the kitchen after she returned home one day in early March 1981. He bashed her head in with a frying pan, crushing her skull, then he and Suzan stabbed her more than a dozen times, mostly in the face and neck. The two wrapped the victim's body in a blanket and placed her in the basement after the gruesome assault. They positioned Keryn's body as if she were sleeping, placing a pillow beneath her head, and then drew various drawings on the walls. In one of the drawings, they also included the name "Suzan."

The End of the Crusade

After they murdered Keryn and left her corpse, the Bear couple ran away and spent some time in hiding. They ran to Oregon and would hunker down near Grants Pass in a forest cabin for some time, in a locale Suzan would refer to as "Allah's mountain." Suzan and Michael stayed in the area until spring of 1982. While in the wilderness, the couple ran into another man who let them take refuge with him, but he eventually turned against them once he got acquainted with their strange and aggressive ways. They later robbed this man and left for Alderpoint, California. The main reason for this move was that they simply got bored in their self-imposed exile.

In California, Suzan and Michael found work on a marijuana farm as manual laborers in Humboldt County in May of 1982. Other farm employees later observed that the Bear couple was consistently strange, advocating anarchist and revolutionary ideas while also preaching their form of Islam and predicting the impending nuclear apocalypse.

Meanwhile, the police were investigating the murder of Keryn Barnes, working on several clues. They soon questioned one of Keryn's friends, who told them the story of Keryn's former roommates and how strange they were. The investigators soon spoke to Keryn's mother, who gave them the couple's self-given names, but those weren't enough for the police to identify and locate them. Nonetheless, Keryn's former roommates were now prime suspects, and it was only a matter of time before the police would identify them.

Back on the farm in Humboldt County, the crusading couple had already made enemies, particularly in a 26-year-old guy named Clark Stephens. He was reportedly too loud for the Bears' liking and a heavy drinker, both of which upset Suzan's supposed Islamic beliefs. Suzan tried to stop Clark from entering the farm one morning, and he responded in his normal loud fashion, hurling a lot of verbal abuse at Suzan. This was a capital offense, according to the couple's beliefs, and Clark was branded a witch as a result.

As before, Suzan left it to Michael to dole out Clark's punishment, so he shot him in the face. The couple then attempted to dispose of Clark's body by burning his corpse with kerosene and burying the remains under chicken waste in the woods. The couple's attempt to conceal the remains worked for a while, and Clark was reported missing after around two weeks. The Humboldt County sheriff's office soon dispatched investigators around the farm, and they eventually found Clark's remains. The Bears, however, had already fled by that point. They had made themselves the prime suspects in yet another murder, though, and the noose was slowly tightening.

The police investigated what remained of the couple's possessions at the farm, but none of the clues were useful as to their possible whereabouts. The investigation hit a turning point in November of 1982 when Michael was spotted by an old acquaintance while hitchhiking around Los Angeles. The police managed to track him down and arrest him, but he was eventually released owing to a bureaucratic mistake. He thus ran free before the investigators from Humboldt County could question him. The police did manage to get some valuable evidence, such as his information and the murder weapon used on Clark.

While on the run, Suzan and Michael headed north again to hide in the mountains. They eventually settled down in another hiding place, where they spent the vast majority of their time, only heading into a local town for necessary supplies. To get there, they would often hitchhike when luck would allow them to do so. In January of 1983, the couple hitched a ride near Bakersfield when they made a fateful encounter with Jon Charles Hellyar, a 30-year-old driver heading to Santa Rosa.

For some reason, Suzan believed right away that Jon was a witch, telling Michael that they would have to kill him. The Bears immediately made for a tense atmosphere as soon as they got in the truck, with Suzan finding an excuse when Jon's leg allegedly touched hers, which she interpreted as an assault and offense deserving of death. A struggle ensued, Jon pulled the truck over to the side of the highway, exited, and the fight continued outside, with several motorists driving by and witnessing the incident. While Suzan stabbed the man, Michael was able to grab Jon's gun and shot him. Jon stayed alive for a while, but he died in the hospital later. The police had already been tipped off to what was going on by the time the couple got into the truck and drove away. After a highway chase, the Bears crashed the car and were finally arrested.

In line with their unhinged and by now entirely psychotic worldview, the couple had little interest in discussing their guilt or innocence. Instead, they asked for a press conference in order to confess to the three murders, which they used to drone on about their bizarre religion for hours. After they described themselves as "vegetarian Moslem warriors" in an interview given to journalists, they were given the name of "the San Francisco Witch Killers." The couple was also suspected of being involved in a dozen additional murders, not only in the United States but also in Europe. They were found guilty of all three murders committed between 1981 and 1983 and were sentenced to life imprisonment, where they remain unremorseful to this day.

CHAPTER THREE

Paul Bernardo and Karla Homolka

Between 1987 and 1990, the Scarborough area of the Canadian city of Ontario was the location of a string of rapes and sexual assaults. Paul Kenneth Bernardo, the perpetrator of these attacks, kept his criminal activities limited to sexual offenses during that time. His violent urges escalated between 1990 and 1992 after he started dating Karla Leanne Homolka.

While Paul had been on this path for quite some time before meeting Karla, she would play a direct role in his subsequent crimes. The couple targeted strangers, but one of the victims would also be Karla's own younger sister. The case would acquire significant notoriety during the subsequent court proceedings, particularly because of Karla's sentence, which was perceived by many as too light, considering her crimes. The leniency by the prosecution, which was something she didn't show any of her victims, was the result of a plea bargain. This was one of the most important aspects of the case since Karla was successful in convincing the court that she, too, was a victim of abuse and an unwilling accomplice in her husband's monstrous crimes. This claim would later fall into question in the light of new evidence, but only after the fact.

Background and a History of Rape

Paul Bernardo was perhaps yet another textbook example of a horrible offender destined for such a dark path since early childhood. He was born in Toronto on August 27, 1964, into what appeared to be a string of fortunate circumstances. The family was wealthy, but there was a sinister side to them that was subsequently revealed. Marilyn, Paul's mother, was adopted but raised in a successful and loving family by Gerald Eastman, a wealthy lawyer, and his wife, Elizabeth. Kenneth, Paul's father, was born into a wealthy family but was raised in an abusive atmosphere. Kenneth Bernardo was scarred by these events, and he grew up with a lot of the same tendencies. Perhaps out of protest, Kenneth chose not to enter his immigrant father's prosperous business and instead sought a career as an accountant.

Paul Bernardo was born after Marilyn began an affair with an ex-boyfriend, but Kenneth reacted with tolerance and accepted being listed as Paul's biological father without a paternity test. The couple had two other children, a boy, and a girl, before these events. Kenneth took after his father and was an abusive father and husband. His problematic behavior culminated in 1975 when he was caught molesting a young girl. It later came to light that he also molested his daughter. Kenneth had a firm hold over the family, though, and Marilyn was unable to garner the strength to fight back. She eventually all but resigned from the family not by moving away but by shutting herself off in the basement of the family's home in Scarborough.

On the surface, young Paul Bernardo handled the abusive home environment better than his older siblings. He never appeared emotionally or psychologically disturbed and was instead known as a happy and adorable child who won many hearts with his smile. He wasn't just a child that seemed nice, though. Paul was remembered by everyone as a well-mannered and polite young boy, who was also a good student. This came to an end when he was sixteen, and his mother informed him that he was not his father's biological son. This realization left a lasting impact on Paul, and he reacted with disgust, accusing his mother of dishonor and openly calling her a "whore."

Family relationships deteriorated, as did Paul's regard for women, but he continued performing well in school, and he stayed the course. He graduated in

1987 from Sir Wilfrid Laurier Collegiate Institute, and he quickly sought employment, beginning as an accountant. He worked for Amway, where he developed a strong interest in sales and began to direct his career toward it. He read books, watched documentaries, and constantly learned how to improve his sales skills. Paul and his friends began using the strategies he learned on ladies during their nights out. He found success with women, but it only helped to deepen his contempt for them, sowing the seeds of dark fantasies and increasingly aggressive behavior.

Paul eventually started attending the University of Toronto Scarborough, at which point he began to externalize some of his fantasies. Apart from just being generally abusive and beating the women he dated, he also drew pleasure from humiliating them, particularly in public. This behavior came to a temporary halt when Jennifer Thompson, a girl he was dating at the time, told him that she would report him to the police. In May of 1987, Paul had already raped two women, and in July, he attempted to rape yet another one, although unsuccessfully. This was only the beginning of Paul's three-year series of sexual assaults, rapes, and batteries.

Bernardo first met Karla Homolka in October of 1987 when she was only 17 while Paul was 23, and the two immediately felt a great attraction to each other. Right from the start, however, this relationship was toxic. The two had intercourse that same night in the presence of their friends. This turned into a long-term relationship, and Paul would routinely visit Karla at least twice a week. Paul treated Karla as a possession, to which she responded with affirmation. He had a hold over Karla and her behavior, including her clothing, diet, mentality, associations, and most other areas of her life. On top of that, insults and humiliation were a common theme of their relationship. All the while, Karla only emboldened Paul, especially his sexual deviancies. Paul was notably furious and seething with jealousy when he learned that he wasn't Karla's first, but the two continued dating.

Bernardo continued his predatory indiscretions, stalking, attacking, and raping numerous other women. His sexual assaults were so frequent that the police took notice of a serial rapist, dubbing him the Scarborough Rapist. A special team of investigators was put together with the sole purpose of apprehending the perpetrator, but the investigation was off to a very slow start. Karla, on the other hand, was well aware that her boyfriend was a serial rapist. In the course of their investigation, the police interviewed one of the victims who claimed that a girl, Karla, was present during her rape. She said that Karla was there to watch and to film the attack, but the police didn't pursue this clue very long.

In May of 1990, the police ultimately decided to release the composite sketch of the assailant, which they had in their possession since 1988. This decision sparked an avalanche of calls and reports from both victims and suspicious citizens. When the investigators discovered they couldn't physically process all of the reports flooding in, one of their previous concerns about the sketch came true. Paul's friends, acquaintances, and ex-girlfriends were among the tips, but most of their information was buried under all the other calls. In November, the cops finally found themselves on Paul's trail, and they obtained warrants to take DNA samples from him, which took two years to process and compare to samples obtained from victims. In 1990, Paul was also already involved in other criminal activities, making much of his income by smuggling cigarettes from and to the US, especially after he left his regular job.

Violent Escalation

Karla herself also had a disturbing background and quite a few personal issues, just like Paul. She was born Karla Leanne Homolka and was the eldest child born to Dorothy and Karel Homolka, who had two other daughters, Lori and Tammy, who were born in 1971 and 1975, respectively. While she was growing up, Karla witnessed a lot of discord between her parents, and her home environment was far from idyllic.

Already by her teens, Karla sought part-time work at a pet shop with the long-term perspective of becoming a veterinarian. At that time, she was in Secondary School in St. Catharine's, Ontario. After graduating from high school, she quickly found work as a veterinary assistant at an animal clinic. She met Paul Bernardo through her job since she traveled to Scarborough for a pet store convention and slept at the same hotel as Paul. Karla was known for declaring her love for animals, but her actions suggested otherwise, such as when she threw a friend's hamster out the window for no apparent reason. At a very young age, Karla began to express some dark interests, such as in crime stories and eventually other topics like the occult and all things death-related.

By 1990, Paul was still obsessed with the fact that his girlfriend had not been a virgin before meeting him. While their relationship continued, he certainly made it no secret that this was a major source of frustration for him. It was at that time when Paul began to take notice of Karla's 15-year-old sister, Tammy, making her the object of many perverted ideas in his head. At that point, Paul and Karla began to plot the rape and murder of the girl. Karla's reaction to such an idea was to contribute by making sure that Tammy would remain a virgin in the meantime and eventually use her veterinary connections to get drugs that they could use to knock Tammy out.

They first tried this on July 24 when Tammy came along on a summer vacation. Karla acquired valium that the couple then used on Tammy's food, but the attempted rape was ultimately unsuccessful because

Tammy woke up after about a minute. Karla's next idea was to "gift" Tammy's virginity to Paul for Christmas, so the couple hatched a new sinister plot to try again after a family Christmas dinner at the Homolka residence on December 23.

Later that evening, when Karla's parents went to sleep, she and Paul put a high dose of sleeping pills into Tammy's drink. This time, it worked, and when Tammy passed out, the couple took her clothes off, after which Paul proceeded to rape the girl. While they were filming the incident, Karla assisted him by holding a rag drenched in a veterinary anesthetic to her face. The anesthetic, Halothane, caused unconscious Tammy to start vomiting and choking while the two assailants tried to clear her throat. Soon enough, Tammy stopped breathing.

When they realized that their victim had died, Paul and Karla immediately began trying to hide the evidence, dressing Tammy's corpse and leaving it in her room before calling the emergency services. Although Tammy had evident chemical burns on her face, police investigators, in a display of some sloppiness, failed to conduct a toxicological examination to discover if there were any drugs in her system. Tammy wasn't spared the couple's perversion even at her funeral, where Paul was seen touching her hair as she lay in the open casket. When Tammy was exhumed during the eventual homicide investigation, the police found that

Karla and Paul had placed a photograph of themselves in Tammy's coffin. It was a photo of the two of them together, smiling as Paul waves at the camera as if to say "bye-bye."

Not long after Tammy's funeral, Paul and Karla moved away to Port Dalhousie to live together. While there, they continued to engage in all manner of debauchery, particularly about Tammy. They used their camera to film themselves having sex while roleplaying reenactments of their rape of Tammy, with Karla acting as her own dead sister. To make it more believable, she even wore some of Tammy's clothes that she still had.

It wasn't long until the couple's sexually murderous appetite kicked in again, and on June 7 of 1991, they struck again. This time, Karla wanted to use a teenage girl for another rape, and for this, she chose a young girl whom she met at work and was friends with. Karla had made up her mind to go outside for the next victim instead of, as she put it regarding Tammy, "minimizing the risk by keeping it in the family." The girl's name was never published, and she remained as "Jane Doe" throughout the trial because she was lucky enough to survive the ordeal. Karla slipped Halcion into the girl's drink after luring her to her and Paul's house, and she passed out. After that, she informed Paul that she had a wedding gift for him, which was a drugged girl for him to rape.

Culmination and Apprehension

The couple filmed their rape of Jane Doe, and they both participated, starting with Karla as the rapist and Paul with the camera. The following morning, the girl woke up thinking that her horrible feeling of nausea was a hangover, having no idea that she had been raped the last night. Two months later, the couple had the same girl visit their home once again, and they drugged her in the same way. This time, however, she stopped breathing at one point as Paul and Karla were assaulting her, at which point Karla made an emergency call. When it turned out that the girl was still alive, Karla called the emergency services again to cancel the ambulance.

Back in June, just around one week after their first rape of this girl, Paul and Karla had already murdered another young girl. This unfortunate 14-year-old was simply at the wrong place, at the wrong time, running into the wrong man. Bernardo himself came to the neighborhood of Burlington as a mere detour on June 15, looking to steal people's license plates to be used on his car while smuggling cigarettes. While he was doing this late at night, 14-year-old Leslie Mahaffy was just coming home from a friend's wake. She found herself locked out of her home and, at first, didn't want to wake her mother so she went to a payphone to call a friend and see if she could stay with them. This didn't work out, at which point Leslie decided to go back to her front door and knock to be let in.

While on her way, Leslie ran into Paul and asked him for a cigarette, which was just the thing he needed to lure her to the back of his car. He blindfolded her and forced her into his vehicle as she approached, driving her home to Port Dalhousie. When he got home, Paul informed Karla that he brought a new "playmate" for them. Probably intending to just rape and then release her, they kept Leslie blindfolded during the sexual assault. The tape of this savage rape and torture was shown, in full, to the court during the subsequent trial, leaving those present simply stunned and some of the lawyers involved with the case permanently traumatized.

At one point during the attack, the victim's blindfold seemed to slip somewhat. This worried the rapists because of the possibility that they could be identified, which was why they decided to kill her the following day. Leslie was fed an overdose of Halcion by Karla, according to Paul's testimony. Karla, on the other hand, said that Paul strangled Leslie to death. Paul claimed that Karla was the one who pushed for the killing since she was the one worried about the blindfold. They kept the body in the basement all day, even inviting the Homolka family over for dinner while the corpse was hidden in the house.

After they were left alone again, Karla and Paul used a circular saw to cut Leslie's body into pieces, which they then tried to conceal into cement blocks. They then threw these cement blocks into Lake Gibson but were unable to do so with the heaviest one, which was left on the shore and subsequently found by a fisherman. This block of cement, which contained Leslie's body pieces, was discovered on June 29, 1991, the day Paul and Karla got married.

On April 16 of 1992, the now-married couple kidnapped another victim, 15-year-old Kristen French. This time, Paul didn't spend a long time stalking his victim before striking at an opportune moment. Paul and Karla simply drove around in broad daylight during after-school hours in St. Catharine's. They found solitary Kristen French walking home and, after pretending they were visitors in need of directions, used a knife to force her into their car. Although they thought they had caught a girl all by her lonesome, there were witnesses this time.

Kristen's parents were quick to react to their daughter's unusual absence, and they got in touch with the police, prompting a search. Witnesses stepped in, and the cops were on a hot trail, but unfortunately, not quickly enough. The Bernardo couple brought Kristen home, where they raped and tortured her for three days over the Easter weekend, filming their crimes as before. This time, the victim was not blindfolded, which the prosecution used to argue that this time, Karla and Paul had planned to murder this girl after having their way with her. They didn't put that much effort into the disposal of the corpse this time. Kristen's tortured, raped, sodomized, and naked body was simply dumped in a ditch in Burlington, where it was eventually found on April 30 of 1992. Not long after this murder, Karla and Paul sought to change their last name to Teale, inspired by a serial killer from Criminal Law, a 1988 movie.

A month after the couple murdered Kristen, Paul was interviewed by the police, and he again avoided becoming the main suspect. By December, the Bernardos' marriage was in shambles, as Paul had grown increasingly abusive with Karla. After he brutally beat her with a flashlight in late December, she initially lied to the police but eventually admitted to having been beaten by her husband, at which point she decided to press charges against Paul. Also, at this time, the police finally matched Bernardo's DNA samples to several rape cases in Scarborough.

Even though the police weren't about to arrest them for the murders, Karla decided to strike preemptively, beginning to tell her family and others that Paul alone killed the girls, at which point she sought to acquire immunity from prosecution. Instead, Karla was given a plea deal in which she was charged only with manslaughter and eventually sentenced to only twelve years in prison. Paul was imprisoned for life with virtually no chance of ever being released, while Karla was released from prison in 2005 to a lot of public outrage. She is now married in Montreal and has had three children with her husband, Thierry Bordelais.

CHAPTER FOUR

Henry Lee Lucas and Ottis Toole

Although it is not common, certain serial killers have been known to confess to hundreds, if not thousands, of unproven murders. They do it for a variety of reasons, including to confuse the police and cause a ruckus, but it can be a matter of ego for others. They consider a high number of victims to be an outstanding achievement that should be sought; thus, they are more than willing to confess.

Although his confirmed number of murders is much lower than the one he claimed, Henry Lee Lucas, like his accomplice, Ottis Elwood Toole, was a prolific killer and particularly an abuser in that he stayed at large for as long as 23 years, killing and assaulting people. The killers' eventual bogus confessions and exaggerated claims, notably Lucas', sparked widespread controversy and infamy. Lucas, a pathological liar, probably expected the notoriety he received, but his stories had an impact on police work across the United States. The events proved particularly embarrassing for some of the police departments involved in the subsequent investigations after it turned out that they coddled and encouraged these confessions in a misguided attempt to improve their homicide clearance rates.

Destined for Evil

Henry and Ottis both came from traumatizing backgrounds, and their youth was disturbed in more ways than one. These were stories of poverty, depravity, sexual derangement, abuse, and many other traumas that would cause long-term damage to any child. There is no doubt that these experiences in childhood and adolescence played a major part in determining the disturbed, homicidal outcome for these men.

Ottis was born Ottis Elwood Toole on March 5 of 1947, in Jacksonville, Florida. As a child, Ottis was caught numerous times wandering around cemeteries while trying to rob the graves and dig up bones. Aside from that, he was always an awkward person, attracting a lot of negative attention with his strange behavior. Toole's father abandoned the family early on to pursue a life of alcoholism, leaving Ottis in the care of his mother. Toole later described his mother as a deranged woman who wished for him to be a girl, forcing him to wear dresses and insisting on calling him, Susan. Toole's mother was also extremely religious and controlling in ways unrelated to his gender.

Toole was also abused and molested by countless other family members and acquaintances, including neighbors and even his elder sister, according to his testimonies. One of Toole's most horrific cases of molestation involved his father's friend with whom he was allegedly forced to have sex when he was only five years old. Ottis also revealed that his passion for digging around graves emanated from his maternal grandmother, who was a Satanist, and encouraged him to participate in bizarre self-mutilation rituals.

Toole wasn't a bright child, and his intellect bordered on impairment with an IQ of 75. However, Toole also suffered from epilepsy, leading to frequent seizures, and he might have had a range of other disabilities such as dyslexia and ADHD. With these conditions, in addition to his illiteracy, Toole might have obtained a lower score than his actual IQ. Aside from digging around cemeteries and running away from home, Toole began committing arson at a young age. It wasn't long before his mischief escalated to serial arson, and Toole eventually developed a sexual fascination with fire, which would influence the nature of his crimes later in life.

Ottis began to believe he was a homosexual at the age of ten, and according to his subsequent testimonies, he had his first consensual homosexual relationship with a neighbor when he was twelve. Ottis dropped out of school in ninth grade and began to spend even more time away from home. Toole began frequenting gay bars and prostituting himself on the street during this period. Toole allegedly committed his first murder when he was fourteen years old, killing a man who was looking for sex, as he later told the police and the public.

He wasn't caught for this crime, though, and his first run-in with jail time was in the summer of 1964 when he was seventeen and got arrested for loitering. In the late 1960s and early 1970s, Toole continued living the life of a drifter, making some money through prostitution in the Southwestern US. In 1974, Toole found himself living in Nebraska when he was suspected by the police to have killed a 24-year-old girl by the name of Patricia Webb. These suspicions caused him to flee the state and settle in Colorado, where he had the same experience when he became a suspect in the murder of Ellen Holman, a 31-year-old woman killed in October of 1974. Both of these women were shot to death.

Ottis fled yet again, and he eventually returned to Jacksonville in 1975. In early 1976, Ottis married a woman who was 25 years older than him. The marriage ended just three days later, presumably after his wife realized that he was gay. During the subsequent questionings and interviews, Ottis explained that this marriage was part of his strategy to hide his sexual orientation.

Henry's early childhood and youthful memories were just as bad, if not worse, than Toole's. He was born Henry Lee Lucas on August 23 of 1936, in Blacksburg, Virginia. Lucas was born into considerable poverty, living in a simple, one-room cabin. At age ten, Lucas suffered an injury during a fight with his brother, which resulted in him losing an eye. From the earliest age, Lucas was noted as a strange boy, just like Toole. This would have come as no surprise given his home situation. Henry's mother supported herself with prostitution and would sometimes force him to watch her having sex. Just like Toole, Lucas was also forced to dress as a girl and would have to go out in public that way, including his school. According to Lucas, his mom eventually started to prostitute him both to men and women, often while cross-dressed.

Henry's father was a heavy alcoholic who died by freezing to death after he passed out drunk outside of the cabin during a blizzard. Henry couldn't stand living with his mother any longer, so he dropped out of school in sixth grade and left home to live as a drifter, chiefly in Virginia. Henry was renowned for mixing in false confessions with honest ones, thus much of what he stated was later withdrawn or disproven, particularly about his murders. One such confession was of his first murder, which he later repudiated. He claimed that he murdered Laura Burnsley, a seventeen-year-old girl, in 1951 because she had rejected him.

Lucas became a serial burglar throughout his time as a drifter, for which he was eventually apprehended. He was charged with up to fifteen counts of burglary largely in the Richmond area, and sentenced to four years in prison. He was captured again after escaping in 1957, and he didn't leave prison until September of 1959.

A Trail of Blood and Destruction

Although Henry Lucas became a free man in late 1959, he struggled to adjust to his newfound freedom. Henry moved to Tecumseh, Michigan, because he had nowhere else to go and was allowed to reside with his half-sister, Opal. He also attempted to make a positive shift in his life by marrying a woman with whom he had exchanged letters while incarcerated. The couple soon became engaged, but things began to fall apart when Henry's mother, Viola, came to visit and expressed her displeasure with the arrangement.

His mother demanded that Henry breaks off the engagement and return to Blacksburg to be her caretaker in her old age. His refusal led to a series of escalating arguments over the following period, in which Henry's already horrible relationship with his mother deteriorated exponentially. Things culminated on January 11 of 1960, when a physical altercation broke out and, as Lucas told the police, Viola grabbed a broom and hit him over the head with it, to which he reacted by stabbing her. In the commotion, Henry ended up slashing her neck, after which he ran away and left her bleeding on the floor.

When Henry's half-sister came home, she stumbled upon a grizzly sight of her mother lying covered in blood, although she was still alive. However, the ambulance didn't arrive in time and Viola passed away thereafter. Strangely enough, the cause of her death, at least according to the subsequent police report, was determined to have been a heart attack facilitated by the stress of the assault. Henry ran, but he didn't get far, and he was soon apprehended in Ohio. He pled not guilty to murder, claiming that he had killed his mother in self-defense, but the jury threw this version out, and Henry was given 40 years in prison with the possibility of parole, having been found guilty of second-degree murder. Lucas, in a remarkable turn of events, was released from prison in June 1970 because the facility was overcrowded.

After he got his freedom back, Henry quickly went back to his old ways, living as a drifter and moving around. His deviant behavior took another turn in 1971 when he was arrested for the attempted kidnapping of three young schoolgirls and sentenced to five years in prison. When he was released in 1975, Henry finally married another woman with whom he exchanged letters while in prison. Unfortunately, he ended up abusing the woman's daughter and was forced to leave, eventually living with several relatives. He eventually managed to find work in West Virginia and begin yet another relationship, but it fell apart once again for the same reasons.

The fateful encounter and homicidal match between Toole and Lucas happened at some point around 1976. The two instantly became friends, and their relationship soon progressed into a romantic one, after which they moved in together in Jacksonville, Florida. Henry then went through a time of relative stability in which he worked, mostly fixing people's roofs and cars. While living in Jacksonville, Lucas got close to Toole's young niece, Frieda Becky Powell, with whom he bonded. She, too, was a kid who struggled in school and had already been in trouble a few times. In 1982, Henry convinced Becky to go to California with him and live the drifter lifestyle.

The two eventually got a job caring for Kate Rich, an 82-old-woman of weak health. They were eventually fired and kicked out when it turned out they weren't doing a very good job and were instead taking money from Rich. In time, Henry and Becky started falling out as Becky wanted to return to Florida, contrary to

Henry's wishes. Things escalated over time until Becky disappeared one day. Henry confessed to killing both Becky and Kate Rich after being arrested on a gun charge in June 1983. He cut Becky up into pieces and scattered her across a field in Denton, Texas. As for Kate Rich, Henry incinerated her body around one month after the murder, during which time it was hidden in a drainage pipe.

Meanwhile, Ottis Toole was doing his own killing, such as in January of 1982 when he locked George Sonnenberg inside his house, which he then set on fire. The 65-year-old man somehow survived the inferno, but he succumbed to his injuries a week later. This was one of the numerous cases of arson and murder that Ottis would talk about with glee after his incarceration, frequently bursting into laughter in interviews and talking about the great sexual arousal that he would always feel when burning things, especially people. Toole was arrested for another crime in the spring of 1983, after which he confessed to the murder of Sonnenberg, claiming it was the result of a lovers' quarrel. This was the least of the gruesome confessions to come.

Confessions and Epilogue

While in custody, Henry initially assisted the police in locating the remains of Frieda Becky Powell and Kate Rich, earning him some credibility with the police investigators. Henry began to recount his wild stories at this point, eventually claiming to have killed about 600 people. Toole, on the other hand, claimed to have assisted Lucas in more than a thousand murders. Two months after Toole's arrest, Henry Lucas was also apprehended, and the two were initially out of sync in terms of their involvement with each other and the killings.

This quickly changed, though, and they then engaged in what could best be described as a confession rampage. In more ways than one, the police ended up encouraging false confessions, especially from Lucas. For one, the police were happy to pin as many unsolved murders as they could on Lucas, so they eagerly ate up many of his stories. This went so far that the investigators even began giving Lucas access to unreleased information about pending cases, which allowed him to use the details from the police files to make his confessions seem more plausible. In the end, Lucas was suspected of involvement in eleven murders, three of which were proven beyond a reasonable doubt.

Among the corroborated confessions, one of the most horrific cases was the monstrous killing of a six-year-old boy by the name of Adam Walsh in Hollywood, Florida. This boy's disappearance in 1981 devastated his parents and led to a public outcry for his return. Extensive searches and manhunts took place, and the disappearance drew a lot of attention from across the country. As it later turned out, Toole abducted Adam in the parking lot of a mall where he was with his mother. The boy's mom had only a momentary lapse of attention as she looked for articles, and Toole used candy and toys to lure the boy away. The panicked woman immediately called her husband, John Walsh, and a missing person's case was soon initiated.

Toole took the Walsh boy to his car and drove away. It wasn't long until the boy started to feel uneasy and ask to go home, at which point he started crying. According to Toole's confession, he found the crying irritating, so he punched the boy in the face. The child then started crying even louder, at which point Toole began savagely beating him until he lost consciousness. The killer then drove to a secluded area where he murdered the barely-conscious boy by strangulation, after which he cut his head off with a machete. After the murder, Toole only disposed of the body while keeping the head in his car for days, at one point simply forgetting about it. After he realized that he had been driving around with the child's severed head for days, he threw it into a canal he was passing by.

The police eventually caught on to the trail and, after the boy's head was discovered, they even got their hands on Toole's blood-soaked car and impounded it. In yet another bizarre twist, the police misplaced the car, which was arguably the most important piece of physical evidence in the case. Toole was never charged with the murder, and he would spend the rest of his life in prison for other crimes. The absence of tangible evidence due to police incompetence and the overwhelming volume of falsified confessions from both killers prevented Toole from being charged in Adam Walsh's case. It wasn't until 2008, twelve years after the man's death, when the Hollywood police decided that Toole was the perpetrator, proclaiming the case closed. The boy's father had been convinced of Toole's guilt all along, though, like many other people. His confessions and the details he gave did fit into the case, especially when he confessed once more, just before dying.

Toole was found guilty of many other murders, including six confirmed victims. Ada Johnson, a 20-year-old woman abducted in Tallahassee and murdered just outside of Fort Walton Beach, was one of these victims. Along with this killing, Toole confessed to the killing of David Schallart, an 18-year-old hitchhiker whom he picked up not far from Pensacola. The pair may have also killed a cop while committing a store robbery. John McDaniel, a later Jackson County Sheriff, was the son of this officer.

Toole and Lucas described the victims they cannibalized, the corpses they sexually abused, the stores they plundered, the fires they started, and much more in their confessions. They started blaming a satanic cult known as "The Hands of Death," at one point, claiming that the cult had sent them on a mission to sacrifice people and eat their flesh. However, no evidence of this cult's existence was ever discovered by investigators. Both killers were initially given multiple death sentences, but all of these were commuted to life sentences after appeals. Ottis Toole and Henry Lucas both died in prison in 1996 and 2001, respectively.

CHAPTER FIVE

Cindy Hendy and David Parker Ray

When the Toy Box Killer is included on a list of murderers, he's usually one of the few, if not the only one on that list, who hasn't actually been convicted of killing anyone. Indeed, the particularly horrifying thing about this long-time kidnapper, sadist, and rapist is that his terrible crimes, including many suspected murders, took place in the span of almost fifty years. Based on the testimonies of his accomplices, including his ex-girlfriend, Cindy Hendy, the police eventually came to suspect David Parker Ray of as many as sixty killings.

David allegedly perpetrated the murders in Arizona and New Mexico while based in Elephant Butte, New Mexico, several miles to the north of a town called Truth or Consequences. David was dubbed the

Toy Box Killer because of his trailer that functioned as a soundproofed torture chamber, which he referred to as his "toy box." David was an unusually prolific rapist and torturer, kidnapping and holding at least a few girls every year. The horrific captivity in his depraved workshop of horrors would usually last for months, after which, the police presumed, the victims would either be murdered or drugged and abandoned. Apart from the sheer brutality and immense scope of the crimes, another particularly difficult part of the case was the lack of closure for so many of David's victims' families.

The Childhood and Adolescence of a Sadist

David Parker Ray, the main perpetrator and instigator of these horrors was born in the small town of Belen, New Mexico, on November 6, 1939. Belen is a small town to this day, but back in the 1930s, it was a little more than a hamlet. David was born into a poor family that was already unstable and fragmented, and it was only going to get worse as time went on. Cecil and Nettie Ray were the names of David's parents, and he had a younger sister named Peggy.

Given how things turned out, it should perhaps be unsurprising that David Parker Ray had a difficult upbringing and a toxic home environment while he was growing up. That's putting it mildly, though, as his father was an extreme alcoholic who was prone to very violent episodes. David and his younger sister eventually ended up living mostly with their grandfather, Ethan Ray, throughout their childhood. Their grandfather was a strict disciplinarian who instilled discipline in his children. Even though the children were effectively raised by their grandfather, the children's abusive father regularly paid visits, and David continued to have a toxic, troubled, and damaging relationship with him.

When Cecil filed for divorce and, for the most part, abandoned the family when David was ten years old, the choice to send the children to their grandfather was made. David's mother's situation wasn't any better, as she was largely absent and uninvolved in her children's lives. She, too, had a long history of substance abuse with alcohol and other drugs, and there came a point where she simply chose her addictions over her children and effectively left them.

While there is no record of David's grandfather being an alcoholic, he certainly incorporated abusive and physical punishments into his disciplinarian approach. Coupled with that, In addition, on some of these visits, David was subjected to periodical abuse from his father. Cecil was also sexually peculiar, especially for that time, and she made no effort to hide her proclivities from David. When she visited the children at their grandfather's home, Cecil would bring pornographic magazines to give to young David, some of which were extreme in content. They were often magazines with themes such as BDSM, involving hardcore pornography of all stock.

Young David really had no escape from abuse and suffering. Aside from his terrible home life and dysfunctional family, David also had to deal with severe bullying at school for years. The bullying was particularly bad while he was attending Mountainair High School in Mountainair, New Mexico. By this time, he was fairly reclusive and especially shy around girls, making it difficult for him to make friends and encouraging bullies to pick on him.

It was also during his high school years that David got started on his road toward trouble. As he grew and became cognizant of his sexuality, he began to develop some very warped ideas and attractions. The initial fascination with BDSM and pornography gradually devolved into real-life sadomasochistic fantasies and thoughts of rape, torture, and murder of women for his own pleasure. During this time, David also started following in his parents' footsteps regarding substance abuse, engaging in experimentation with both drugs and alcohol.

Eventually, David's sister stumbled upon his stash of pornography and other disturbing material such as BDSM photography. The stash also contained David's drawings, which portrayed many sexually disturbing scenes. David was in early high school, so he was only around fourteen during this time, so David's younger sister was quite disturbed by what she saw. Being a loyal sister, however, Peggy chose to keep her discovery a secret and cover for her brother, and she wouldn't talk about any of this until the eventual legal proceedings against David, decades later.

David likely developed a significant hatred for women during his adolescence, based on a mixture of factors such as the absence of his mother in childhood and the rejection that he experienced as a recluse. It was that very rejection or, rather, his inability to find a girlfriend that was often the very reason why he got bullied and tormented. In a way, this probably made young David associate women not just with rejection but also cruelty. The early warning signs that a sadistic and violent nature was forming within David were clearly there, but they went under the radar. It wasn't just that his sister kept his proclivities quiet, though, since David was simply good at hiding them most of the time. Despite being peculiar, none of his strangeness ever manifested in delinquency, and David would rarely if ever, get into trouble at school. This was good enough as far as his teachers were concerned, so he was never perceived as anything more than just a kid who was a bit quiet.

After David finished high school, he enlisted in the military and served as a mechanic before being honorably discharged. During these years, David's life still showed some semblance of normalcy and potential for a positive outcome. From his teenage years, till he was older, he worked as a mechanic in various capacities for most of his life. While doing so, David honed his skills as a mechanic, which was later corroborated by numerous testimonies. David was also a very skilled and crafty man, who would often make his special tools to help him get the task done faster and better, a skill that would come in handy in his crimes.

Ray was an overall productive and diligent worker who was very committed to his job but also to help others. He was noted as a good teacher who had no problem passing on his knowledge and skills to others who wanted to get into his trade. Beyond work, people generally viewed David as a friendly individual who was always available to lend a helping hand.

A Secret Life Hidden in Plain Sight

David had been evolving into a monster for a long time, hiding behind his friendly facade of an upstanding worker and community member. In his youth, it wasn't long until David got married to the first of his eventual four wives. David eventually told his first wife a story about some of his early experiments with actual violence and how he began to act on his fantasies, as his first wife later testified. He told her that he abducted a woman for the first time in his life when he was still in his early teens. According to the narrative, David then tied the woman to a tree in a secluded area and tormented her before killing her.

David's wife kept quiet about it because she thought her husband was just a traumatized young man who might be suffering from mental illness. For these reasons, she assumed he made up the scenario and was simply talking out loud about another of his depraved, sadistic fantasies. And so, David's first confession was mostly brushed off. In time, however, David's behavior grew increasingly bizarre to a point where his first wife, as tolerant as she was, could no longer take it and they eventually divorced. Whether his story about his first kill was true or not, David started indulging in crime during adolescence, especially after high school.

Even though all four of David's marriages would end in divorce, he did have something to show for them in the form of his two children - a boy in 1960 and a daughter in 1969 - in two different marriages. The daughter would eventually turn into an accomplice in many of her father's crimes and would play an important role in the case. By his 50s, David had spent his years getting by and hiding in plain sight. He worked, his family life went through ups and downs, and, for the most part, he lived as normally as one could expect, given his background. David had undoubtedly started his long-term crime spree well before he was in his 50s, though, at some point beginning to kidnap, torture, rape, and presumably kill women. On the surface, though, David was still that regular, helpful guy just trying to make the best of his circumstances for all those years, but by the fifth decade of his life, his sadistic secret life was certainly reaching a culmination.

At this time, David was living in the town of Elephant Butte in New Mexico, not far from Truth or Consequences. For a time, the area around Elephant Butte and Truth or Consequences was a relatively nice place, owing largely to the local manmade reservoir. Since its creation, the lake was an important landmark in this generally desert area, quickly making it popular with people looking to retire in this part of New Mexico. Unfortunately, the area was also attractive to all kinds of drifters, including drug addicts, prostitutes, dealers, and others. Many of these drifters and regular homeless people started to gather around the lake, setting up camps and shanty settlements, which eventually led to a great uptick in criminal activity. This region had one of the highest rates of rape in the country in the late 1990s, as well as other forms of crime.

By 1986, David's daughter, born Glenda Jean Ray but usually going by Jesse Ray, was well aware of her father's kidnapping, torture, and rape of women. She had a very close relationship with her father and even mimicked him in many ways. Since the day she was born, David treated her more or less as a favorite, at least until the time when he eventually abandoned his family, as he had done before. This was also roughly the time when David settled down on Bass Road in Elephant Butte, not far from the reservoir, with his then-wife Joni-Lee.

Over the years, David had managed to save up a decent sum of money, but he didn't use it to buy a house, invest in a business, or anything else of that nature. He did acquire some basic properties, but David had a different kind of dream for all his life, and that dream was to build his personal torture chamber and depraved sex dungeon, which he named "toy box." To buy the trailer and retrofit it with all manner of sex toys and torturous contraptions and devices, David would spend a total of around $100,000. Cindy Hendy, whom David had been dating for a while at the time, assisted him in this and all subsequent grizzly ventures during the 1990s. After his fourth divorce, David met Cindy while working as a mechanic at Elephant Butte Lake State Park, and the two started dating. During that time, Cindy did some work there as well, although it was mostly community service.

Disturbing Revelations

David's "toy box" was his dream but everyone else's nightmare. He went to great lengths to equip the trailer with as many appliances as possible, indicating a terrifying level of commitment to inflicting pain for his personal sexual gratification. Aside from the usual sex toys, work tools, and surgical equipment that could be used to harm or kill people, David used his ingenuity and mechanical know-how to build tools, machines, and some very intricate contraptions, all for the purpose of sexual torture. Spiked sex toys, whips, chains, shackles, a fur-lined coffin, batteries, electrocution clamps, and other customized sex toys were among the items discovered in the trailer.

David also managed to procure a gynecological examination table, which was the centerpiece of the torture chamber and was modified to suit a new, depraved purpose. There were also various machines, notably penetration machines, which David had built with his own hands so that he would have something that could automatically jab into his victims. The interior of the trailer was covered almost entirely in pornographic material extracted mostly from magazines, while the ceiling had mirrors that were placed there so the victims could see themselves while being tortured and abused. On top of that, David built a wooden frame that served as a pillory, keeping the victim hunched over and restrained. Whenever he sends his accomplices or animals such as dogs to rape whoever was held captive, he would often use this to keep victims in position.

The torturer's method of operation often involved impersonating an undercover cop, which not only allowed him to manipulate people under duress but also provided him with easy access to prostitutes. David would regularly hire prostitutes, whom he would then abduct under the guise of being arrested for prostitution. This is exactly what David was up to with an Elephant Butte prostitute by the name of Cynthia Vigil Jaramillo in March of 1999. This fateful encounter would lead to the case that would bring about the unraveling of David's long-time spree of horror, finally letting the world see this man for what he truly was.

It all began when Cynthia was seen running down a street in Elephant Butte on a particular morning in March of 1999. She was bloodied, naked, and wearing a metal slave collar, running frantically and in a daze, making a desperate dash toward freedom. The girl had been kept chained to a bed in the living room of David's and Cindy's home for three days before she saw her opportunity to get away while David was at work and Cindy, who was supposed to supervise the captive, was on the phone in another room. Cindy had mistakenly left the keys to the lock on Cynthia's chain close by on a table, and this would cost the torturous couple dearly. Cindy caught Cynthia in the act of escape, which led to a struggle that resulted in Cindy getting stabbed with an icepick.

A Good Samaritan eventually took Cynthia in, helped her, and informed the police. A string of arrests soon followed, leading to the apprehension of David Ray, Cindy Hendy, and others. The investigation quickly revealed additional accomplices, including, at least, David's daughter Jesse and a friend by the name of Dennis Yancy. Angelica Montano was one of the many victims who came forward after the case became widely publicized. Apart from the unwillingness of many victims to testify, another problem was David's fairly successful use of drugs to induce amnesia in his victims. Some of them later had difficulties discerning whether their experiences had been real or just nightmares.

Some victims, such as Kelli Garrett, were only identified after the FBI found videotapes that David had made while torturing his captives. Garrett was only identified and brought forward in the subsequent proceedings because the FBI investigators managed to identify her tattoo from the footage. As it turned out, Garrett was drugged and lured by Jesse Ray in Truth or Consequences, after which David brought her to his torture chamber. At one point, David tried to kill her by cutting her throat and dumping her by the road, but she miraculously survived. Unfortunately, neither the cops nor Garrett's husband believed her story, and she ended up not only ignored by the police but even divorced by her husband, who believed that she had been out cheating on him that night. The torturers also imprisoned and abused a former girlfriend of Dennis Yancy, Marie Parker, whom Dennis eventually strangled while David filmed.

David also made audio recordings during his many torture sessions, as he particularly enjoyed announcing to his victims what sort of horror he had in store for them, taking pleasure in the psychological terror that he inflicted. Investigators later found that David had probably created snuff films as well, which he would sell. Many of David's alleged murders came to light as a result of Cindy's confessions and testimonies, which were part of her plea deal.

David too eventually entered a plea deal, which resulted in zero murder charges but ended up giving Ray a total of 224 years in prison for a range of other charges. Based on physical evidence and Cindy's cooperation, the police confirmed a total of 14 murders attributed to Ray while officially suspecting more than 60. The prosecutors were content to put Ray away for 224 years on other convictions, so they didn't pursue the murders any further in court. He died of a heart attack in May of 2002, just before he was supposed to be questioned by the New Mexico State Police concerning some open investigations. His daughter, Jesse Ray, was also eventually arrested, charged, and convicted of kidnapping, ending up in prison for only two and a half years. Cindy, on the other hand, was sentenced to 36 years in prison but was granted parole in July of 2019 and is now a free woman.

CHAPTER SIX

Carol Bundy and Doug Clark

The case of Doug Clark and his girlfriend, Carol Bundy, is a story of how shockingly fast a disturbed individual's fantasies can escalate, become externalized, and then get even worse. From consensual sexual experimentation with prostitutes to pedophilia to murder, Dough Clark and his accomplice shocked California with a series of murders in a matter of months in 1980. The abductions and horrible killings that the two committed quickly earned them a couple of different names, such as "The Sunset Strip Killers," "The Sunset Strip Slayers," and "The Hollywood Slashers."

A sick fascination with death and sex quickly spiraled into necrophilia, and the already horrific murders only got a whole lot worse. Carol Bundy may have initially had misgivings and could have even been close to turning on her boyfriend, but she ultimately gave in, and quite willingly so. Her eventual and final change of heart would come too late, only after the two had already left a trail of blood in their wake. Neighborhood children, prostitutes, and eventually witnesses were all targeted by Carol and Doug, with Doug's twisted and deranged sexual appetite being the driving force behind most of the crimes.

Backgrounds and the Lead-Up to Killings

Carol was the deranged killer with a troubled past and upbringing, whereas Doug came from an opposite set of circumstances. Carol Mary Peters was born on August 26, 1942, to Charles and Gladys Peters as one of their three children. Carol's experience with family life was one filled with alcoholism and abuse from the earliest age, which she was subjected to from both of her parents. Her mother passed away when Carol was just eleven years old.

Carol was not only greatly affected by her mother's death, but her home situation deteriorated even worse when her father added sexual abuse to the list of burdens Carol would have to bear at home. Despite all this, Carol developed a strange coping mechanism in which she would completely idealize her childhood for years, creating what could almost be considered a parallel reality that she could escape to when reflecting on her past later in life. Psychiatrists would have to work very hard to break through to Carol and convince her that her delusions simply weren't true. Simply put, Carol was convinced that she had a very happy childhood, and she developed a selective memory that would isolate, emphasize, and sometimes embellish all the happy moments that she remembered. Carol's favorite memories to share were some happy Christmases that she remembered.

She was particularly adamant in her idealization of her mom. In her recollections, Carol gave her mother a sheen of glamour and beauty that were worthy of a fairytale. Carol seemed to also envy her mother or, rather, the false image of her mother that she had instilled in her own mind. Carol's memory of her mother's death was also heavily idealized, dramatized, and fairly bizarre. Carol's father eventually remarried, after which the abused girl was neglected even more, eventually going through several foster homes. Carol was only 17 when she first got married – to a 56-year-old man. By the time she met Doug Clark in 1979, Carol had gone through three different marriages, all of which she had fled after experiencing abuse. It was during her third marriage that she had two sons.

Doug Clark was born Douglas Daniel Clark on March 10 of 1948 and was the son of Franklin Clark, a Naval Intelligence officer with a successful career. Due to the nature of his father's job, Doug's family had to often move around, not just around the US but all over the world. Doug would spend time in the Marshall Islands, India, Switzerland, and many other places, living in as many as 37 countries at one point or another. Franklin went through a significant career shift in 1958 when he got retired from the army and started working as a civilian engineer in Texas, but this job, just like the last, involved a lot of moving for the family.

Growing up, Doug had all the privileges that he needed to set him on a path to success. When the time was right, he was enrolled in a prestigious international school in Geneva, Switzerland, and would eventually try to follow in his father's military footsteps when he began to attend Culver Military Academy. Doug's first experience of independence began here, as well, because he went to school while his father worked far away, as usual. For a time, things seemed to be going well for Doug, and he graduated from the academy in 1967, after which he began his career as a US Air Force officer in Ohio and Colorado.

Carol met Doug around the Christmas of 1979 in a bar in North Hollywood where she had gone to follow one of her lovers, John Murray, who performed there as a singer. This man had been the manager of an apartment block where Carol was living after abandoning her third husband, and he was a married man when he began an affair with Carol. During the affair, Carol made efforts to end his marriage by bribing the man's wife, which resulted in her getting evicted from the apartment block.

By this time, Doug had already been discharged from the military, after which he was forced to find other work, starting in a soap factory in Burbank, California. This was when he started using his well-traveled mannerisms, intelligence, and charm to develop a system of manipulation and deception that he would use on particular women. He would find women who were overweight, unattractive, and lonely, and he would quickly infiltrate himself into their lives, getting them to pay his rent and feed him while he provided them a dose of attention that they so craved. This attention only went to certain lengths, though, and once these women wanted a firmer commitment, he would just bail and move on to the next one. His approach to 37-year-old Carol was no different, and the two began living together in no time.

The Sunset Strip Slayings

It quickly became apparent that it wasn't just manipulation, though. The two really did click, and there was a lot of understanding between them. The bond started to become particularly strong once Doug and Clark realized that they shared many of the same sexual fantasies, some of which were very dark and depraved.

Doug had been prone to problematic behavior and sexual indiscretions for a long time up that point. He would sometimes record himself having sex with girls without their knowledge as early as his teenage years, but it was just the beginning.

Not long after they moved in together, Clark was already bringing home other women, especially prostitutes. Carol would tolerate these indiscretions and Clark's deviant sexual proclivities, in general. She would also meet every request he had, such as participating in group sex with the prostitutes he would bring home. For Doug, prostitutes were only the beginning, and his appetites were growing fast. After a while, he began to watch and stalk an 11-year-old girl from the neighborhood. Carol then helped Clark get the girl to their apartment, where they made her take off her clothes and pose for pornographic photos with Clark. Carol was seemingly unfazed by Doug's sudden escalation to pedophilia.

She continued tolerating and emboldening Doug's ever-worsening sexual deviancy. In no time at all, Doug was no longer satisfied with just pedophilia but instead began talking about spicing up their sex life even further with things like murder and necrophilia. In graphic detail, Clark told Carol about his new fixation, which was the idea of killing a girl while having sex with her. At the height of his derangement, Doug became interested in what it would be like to shoot a woman in the head during intercourse so that he could feel her contractions at the point of death. For this, he tasked Carol Bundy with procuring pistols for him.

Clark started his killing spree on his own, so Carol was uninvolved in his first murder. His first victims were two teenage half-sisters, Gina Narano and Cynthia Chandler, who had run away from home and disappeared on June 11 of 1980. Gina and Cynthia were 15 and 16 years old, respectively. That night, Clark came home and told Carol how he had abducted the girls on the Sunset Strip and then forced them to perform oral sex on him at gunpoint. He then executed them by shooting each girl in the side of the head with his pistol. He then took them to a garage and proceeded to sexually violate their corpses. The girls' bodies were found the next morning next to the Ventura Freeway, close to Griffith Park, LA.

Carol was seemingly distraught after first hearing about the killings since she tried to turn Doug into the police, to an extent at least. She called the cops and told them that she had information about the crime, but she soon lost her nerve and refused to give any information that could help identify or apprehend the suspect. Clark wasn't particularly upset about this, and he instead used the opportunity to reassure Carol and bring her closer under his wing. He told her that she wouldn't have to worry about repercussions if either of them were ever arrested because he would take all the blame and testify that she wasn't involved in any of his crimes.

Less than two weeks after these initial killings, Clark struck again, this time killing two prostitutes, Karen Jones, and Exxie Wilson. Clark used his usual MO of luring the victims into his car and later shooting them, and this time it was even easier since all he had to do was solicit the services of these prostitutes. Both victims were executed before having their bodies discarded where they could easily be found. Clark went a bit further this time by decapitating Exxie Wilson's corpse after killing her. He took the head as a trophy of sorts and put it in the fridge at home. Carol soon located the head in the fridge, but she had no concerns and was willing to continue. She then adorned the severed head with make-up, later testifying that she and Clark "had a lot of fun" with it. Clark later used the head to indulge in his necrophilia.

After Clark got bored with his unholy toy, the couple cleaned the head off and placed it in a box, after which Clark threw it away in an alleyway. It wasn't long until the head was found and connected to the already-identified remains of Exxie Wilson. By June 27, the local press was already writing about the so-called Sunset Strip Slayer before the police found the box. Only three days after this, the police found the remains of another one of Doug's victims, a girl by the name of Marnette Comer, who ran away from Sacramento sometime before that. The body was found in a forested area of the San Fernando Valley, not far from Sylmar. The investigators determined that the mummified remains of this victim were around three weeks old, making this one Doug's first killings. Marnette was only 17, and she was a prostitute who was often found on the Sunset Strip.

Arrest and the Matter of Guilt

The police found another victim fitting the Sunset Strip Slayer's profile on July 25; a girl labeled as Jane Doe because she couldn't be identified. Her body was found dumped on Sunset Boulevard, executed with a point-blank shot to the head. Another corpse was later found around Fernwood, and although the remains had been mangled and torn to shreds by animals, a skull hole from Doug's signature bullet to the head was clearly visible.

All the while, Carol was still in touch with John Murray, her former apartment manager, and lover. She continued to frequent the establishments where he would perform his country music. Cracks in Carol's conscience began to show when, on one such night, she got drunk and began to spill the grizzly details to Murray, telling him about the things she and her boyfriend were doing. John was shocked, and he started talking to Carol about the possibility of informing the police.

Carol decided to prevent John from ever speaking to the police, even though she was the one who told him and had already attempted to report Doug herself. On August 5, she pretended to want to have sex with him in his van, then shot him and cut off his head. Carol also stabbed Murray multiple times and slashed his hind parts with a knife. Murray's brutalized corpse was found four days later.

Despite the brutality with which she defended Clark, Carol was definitely starting to crack under the weight of her crimes and secrets at this point. Two days after she heard that Murray's corpse was found, perhaps shocked by the new perspective that she got by hearing the grizzly details of her deeds on television, Carol couldn't take it any longer. She broke down in front of a coworker at work and told her about the crimes while sobbing. The woman was shocked by what she heard, and she soon informed the police.

In late August of 1980, the police discovered the remains of another victim in Newhall, California, which they believed was connected to the Sunset Strip Killer. The woman was shot in the head and half-naked, but the police were never able to identify her. The corpse had been skeletonized and decomposed beyond recognition, probably also damaged by wild animals. With the help of experts, they managed to reconstruct her face in an effort to determine what she looked like. The police hoped that her face would lead someone to come forward and recognize her as a missing person, but no such information ever came.

Carol was arrested at her house on the same day she informed her coworkers about the killings and was reported to the cops. They searched the premises right after and discovered all sorts of evidence, including trophies from the victims and photos of Clark torturing the 11-year-old girl the couple had lured into the apartment. Carol began to talk immediately after being taken into custody, and she would eventually make a full confession about her and Clark's misdeeds.

Clark was soon apprehended at his job, where the police found the murder weapons that he had used in most of the killings, and charges soon followed. Carol herself was charged for two murders, including Murray and one of the unidentified victims that the couple killed together. Clark, on the other hand, was charged with six counts of murder and a slew of evidence against him. During the trial, he decided to be his own legal counsel.

One of the distinct characteristics and contention points, in this case, was the matter of who really instigated the crimes and pushed the fantasies over the edge. Specifically, many investigators and observers alike wondered about the extent to which Carol was an accomplice, especially a willing one. On the surface, it's fairly easy to assume that Doug was the main culprit and a manipulator who dragged impressionable and desperate Carol into his murderous spiral, but the fact is that the investigation showed that Carol too was no stranger to lies and manipulation. However, the evidence and the sequence of events that the police investigators were able to put together show us that Doug most likely began killing alone before Carol joined him.

Nonetheless, Clark maintained that he was the one being manipulated and that he didn't want to do any of it. His explanation fell on deaf ears, and the jury found him guilty as charged, and he was sentenced to death in 1983. Carol's claims were disputed by certain specialists, including criminologist Christopher Berry-Dee, who considered Carol's testimony as doubtful because she had been known to falsify details of the narrative multiple times. Furthermore, the court may have given too little credibility to some of Clark's possible alibis for some of the murders. Carol later claimed that the cop allowed her to withdraw a large sum of money from John Murray's bank account, which she said the police took.

Carol was allowed to sign a plea deal as a result of her testimony and confession, but she was ultimately sentenced to 52 years in prison for her role in the Sunset Strip slayings. While Carol died due to heart complications in 2003, Clark, now 73, is still alive on death row in California, pending the conclusion of California's ongoing debate concerning capital punishment. This makes Clark one of 701 prisoners currently waiting for execution in California.

CHAPTER SEVEN

Monique Oliver and Michel Fourniret

Mainland Europe is another place that has had its fair share of experience with criminals of all stock, including serial killers. A notable case was that of the so-called Ogre of the Ardennes, who killed at least eight young girls in a period of fourteen years in the 1980s and 1990s in France and Belgium. His name was Michel Fourniret, and, just like Doug Clark, he too was eventually caught after his wife and accomplice, Monique Pierrette Olivier, decided to tell the police about her husband's terrible crimes.

Michel was able to continue kidnapping and killing for sixteen years until being apprehended, killing possibly twelve or more people. He and his wife both made additional confessions after they had already been convicted and had begun serving their sentences, resulting in an increase in the total number of victims. Later on, Fourniret was also dubbed the "Virgin Hunter" because one of the key aspects of his modus operandi was the rape of women whom he believed to be virgins. This case drew a lot of public attention in France and was the subject of many subsequent public discussions, particularly regarding the legal system. Particularly controversial was Michel's history of incarceration and the fact that he was well-known to the police for all those years during which he preyed on girls.

A Life-Long Fixation

During their self-imposed exile in the Ardennes in the early 1990s, Michel Fourniret and Monique Oliver seemed like a perfectly normal couple to most outside observers. They were quiet and didn't draw any attention in the small village of Sart-Custinne in 1991. They had brought their 3-year-old son with them, and they even managed to find work for a time at a primary school in the area, working as supervisors. This was just one instance that illustrated how adept Michel and Monique, his faithful partner in murder, were at hiding in plain sight despite their horrific secret deeds.

Michel was born on April 4, 1942, in Sedan, France, a village on the border of France and Belgium. He comes from a working-class household because his mother was from a family of farmers and his father worked in the metal industry. His father worked long hours and was usually absent, and he may have been an alcoholic. Michel was quiet and usually a bit of an outsider who didn't make friends easily. He might have had above-average intelligence, and he showed an early interest in things like chess and classical music. Still, his academic performance was average, and Michel simply didn't stick out among his peers for the most part. Eventually, Michel's parents separated, and his father got custody of him and his siblings, a sister and brother, both older.

Michel later said that his mom was an abusive woman who coerced him into a sexual relationship with her, which he said was deeply traumatic for him. He said that this incestuous experience was the driving force behind his eventual violent attitudes toward women. However, during his subsequent interrogations and examinations, most of the experts who worked on the case concluded that Michel likely lied about his mother's abuse. According to Michel, another experience that left a lasting imprint on his mind was the realization that his first wife was not a virgin like he was when they married, which he found deeply disturbing. This was roughly the time when his obsession with virgins became cemented in his mind.

One of the bizarre ideas that Michel had developed about women from an early age was that they don't have to defecate, which he believed to be degrading and beneath them. As he later told, this illusion of his was shattered when he once saw his sister defecating into a bucket when he was young. Michel was fixated on this incident for some reason, and he spoke about it as a source of trauma, which added to his bizarre perception of women. For years as he grew older, Michel would notice more perceived imperfections in women, which he would then contrast in his mind with the concept of a pure, flawless virgin. This idealized, almost mythical construct became increasingly consolidated in his mind over time until he became fully obsessed with it.

There isn't much information documented about Michel's life before his actual crimes, but we do know that he was on his way to normal life at one point. Michel served in the military as a young man and afterward worked at a mill and as a carpenter before primarily becoming a forester. In general, he had several jobs since he found it difficult to stick to one. Michel married for the first time in 1964 and had one child in this marriage. Unfortunately, Michel's sexual obsessions with virgins only kept getting stronger, and he eventually started to act on them, putting a strain on his marriage. In 1967, Michel had his first run-in with the law when he sexually molested a young girl.

Michel's first wife left him not long after his arrest. He remarried in 1970 with his second wife, with whom he had three additional children. Nonetheless, Michel continued down the abyss and would ultimately be arrested again in 1984, having been charged for about a dozen instances of rape, molestation, and sexual assault in the period between 1966 and 1973 alone. Michel was given seven years in prison for his series of attacks. Needless to say, Michel soon found himself divorced yet again.

It was while he was in prison that he met Monique Oliver, first through correspondence. Monique, unlike his first two wives, shared similar interests and agreed with Michel's disturbing sexual beliefs and behavior. She had made up her mind to become his eventual accomplice from the start. Monique was aware that Michel had no intention of becoming rehabilitated or ceasing his illegal activities after being released from prison. So, rather than being horrified by Michel or attempting to persuade him to change his ways, Monique assisted him in devising new techniques to help him escape the law and stay out of prison following his release. In essence, Michel's primary lesson in prison was that he never wanted to be caught again.

The Terrible Pact

At the time, prisoners like Michel were allowed to put adverts in newspapers for several reasons. They could, for instance, put out an advert to invite women from the outside to start some correspondence with them as a way of suppressing the feelings of loneliness and isolation. This was exactly how Michel and Monique first established contact, and Michel soon realized that Monique would be the perfect accomplice. He needed a woman who would encourage him and help him find virgins that he could victimize, and Monique was very willing. The two used their letters to agree on many things that they would do after Michel's release, and they created a sort of pact between them. The pact was a simple agreement that Michel would kill Monique's first husband, and, in exchange, she would help him on his virgin hunt.

Michel never fulfilled his part of this murderous bargain, but this was how he and Monique went from pen pals to marriage and ultimately to partners in horrific crimes. From the get-go, they seemed to be the perfect awful match since Monique, even if she had simply been attracted to convicts, could have chosen several other men. Instead, she chose Michel, and she did so only after learning about his past offenses in detail and confirming his intent to go back to his old ways after release. This illustrates Monique's willingness to participate and the active role that she played in the evil deeds that ensued.

Fourniret was released in 1987, and the first big thing he did was to marry Monique, after which the newlyweds moved to a small town in Burgundy, France. Once they settled in, it didn't take long at all for the couple to get started on their diabolical plans.

In December of 1987, only a couple of months after Michel's release on parole, he and Monique found their first victim. That victim was Isabelle Laville, a 17-year-old girl whom the Fourniret had been stalking for a couple of days before the attack. On that day, Isabelle was walking home from school when Monique came by in her car, offering a lift and asking for directions. After the girl got in the car, Monique drove further down the road, where Michel was waiting, pretending that his car had broken down. Not long after Monique picked Michel up, the two choked and sedated Isabelle in their car, after which they took her home.

Once they got home, Michel raped and then strangled the girl to death as the two had planned. They disposed of her body by throwing it down a well, and Isabelle's remains weren't found until 2006. As per subsequent testimonies, Michel and Monique would reenact these events while having sex many times, with Monique roleplaying as the young girl.

The next murder that the Fourniret's committed wasn't sexual in nature, and it had nothing to do with their perverted virgin hunt. The victim was 30-year-old Farida Hammiche, the wife of a bank robber by the name of Jean-Pierre Hellegouarch, who was Michel's cellmate during his incarceration. In March of 1988, she got in touch with Michel concerning the retrieval of a stash of money that Jean-Pierre had already told Michel about while he was in prison. The stash was supposedly filled with quite a bit of money as well as gold. The information on this treasure's location wasn't very clear, though, so the Fourniret's joined forces with Farida to try and find it together and then split the riches. As it turned out, the stash was very real, and the take amounted to around $1,000,000.

Michel and Monique had no intention of sharing, though. They lured Farida in under the pretense of splitting the money, and then they killed her. Farida's body has never been found. With their newfound wealth, Michel and Monique bought a mansion on a 32-acre property in a very isolated location in the country, which was the perfect setting for them to continue their diabolical hunt for young girls.

Ogre of the Ardennes

In addition, Monique became pregnant with Michel's child in 1988, and the couple planned to use this as a cover for their crimes. Monique had the notion late in her pregnancy to use her condition to easily trick potential victims and lure them in. She had her first opportunity to use her new evil approach in August 1988, when she noticed 20-year-old Fabienne Leroy in the parking lot of a supermarket in Chalons-en-Champagne. Monique approached her, pretending that she wasn't feeling very well and that she might be going into labor and need urgent medical assistance. The true evil of this manipulation was certainly in the abuse of the way every well-adjusted person and society, in general, perceive pregnant women. We aren't conditioned either by nature or nurture to fear women, let alone pregnant women, and when they ask for help, the vast majority of people rightfully feel obliged to assist.

Being perfectly aware of what she was doing, the kindness of a well-intentioned stranger was exactly what Monique had been counting on. Of course, Fabienne was eager to help, and she followed Monique to her car. As soon as Fabienne entered the front seat, Michel got up from the back seat, where he was hiding, and subdued her. The couple then drove their new victim to a remote location and forced her out of the vehicle at gunpoint. Michel allegedly raped and murdered the girl after Monique supposedly checked her to establish her virginity, which Monique denied, and her body was just abandoned in the area and left to rot.

A couple of months after the murder of Fabienne, Monique gave birth to a son who was named Selim. Not even motherhood could soften Monique's cold heart and make her reconsider the things she was participating in, so the couple was soon at it again. Their next victim was Jeanne-Marie Desramault, a 21-year-old girl whom Michel met on a train going to Charleville-Mezieres in January of 1989. Michel and Monique met with Jeanne-Marie again in March, and they invited her to their house for a visit. Michel merely asked his victim if she was a virgin this time, to which she replied that she wasn't and that she was in a relationship. This infuriated Michel and, frenzied, he attacked the girl in an attempt to rape her. Jeanne-Marie managed to free herself in the ensuing struggle and run for the door, but both Michel and Monique quickly caught up and subdued her, after which Michel strangled her.

Michel would strike again just a few days before Christmas that same year, this time attacking a 12-year-old girl. The attack took place just across the border in the Belgian town of Namur, where Michel had been driving with his wife and 1-year-old son. Elisabeth Brichet, a girl on her way to a friend's house when Michel spotted her, was the victim. Michel then waited in the vicinity until the girl returned home in the afternoon. He approached the girl, as he and Monique had done before, and asked her for directions to a doctor that his son needed.

The girl agreed to get in the car and lead them there, after which Michel drove her to his execution site. When they got there, and the Fourniret couple started molesting the girl, Monique examined her and realized that the girl was on her period, at which point she cleaned her and left her until the morning. The following day, they took Elisabeth to their mansion, where Michel first tried to put a bag on the girl's head and suffocate her. After this failed, Michel strangled the victim like most of the others. He and Monique then buried the girl on the property not far from where they buried Jeanne-Marie earlier. The disappearance of Elisabeth sent shockwaves throughout the region, both in France and Belgium. Other people, such as the Belgian serial killer Marc Dutroux, were arrested in connection to Elisabeth's disappearance, but in the 2000s, the truth would come out about the Fourniret's.

In November of 1990, the couple would commit the last murder that they perpetrated together. They went on a shopping trip to the city of Reze, not far from the west coast of France. At the shopping center where they were visiting, the Fourniret's spotted a 13-year-old girl by the name of Natacha Danais in the parking lot. The unfortunate child was there only because her mother forgot her purse in the car and had sent her to get it. The couple used their usual MO to lure the girl and get her in their vehicle, after which they drove out closer to the coast and found an isolated area. This time, Michel first killed the girl by stabbing her with a screwdriver and strangling her, raping her only after she was dead.

To make the tragedy even worse, the spotting of Michel's van as he picked the girl up at the mall later led to the arrest of a neighbor who had a similar van. The man, Jean Groix, was completely innocent of the crime, but he had been on the police radar for a while due to a suspected connection to the Spanish ETA terrorist organization. The cops suspected him of harboring ETA members, and they believed he might have killed the girl after she spotted his activities. Jean Groix later hung himself in prison, being devastated by the accusation of committing this most heinous murder.

Soon after, the Fournirets relocated to the Belgian town of Sart-Custinne, where they remained silent for a time. Michel confessed to killing two more French girls, Celine Saison and Mananya Thumpong, in 2000 and 2001, respectively, during the subsequent court proceedings. The unraveling of this murderous couple began in 2003 when they failed to abduct 13-year-old Marie, who, while tied up in the back of their car, kicked the backdoor open and escaped, only to be picked up by a Good Samaritan. The courageous girl not only got away but even remembered the license plate number on her abductors' vehicle. Initial police investigations and interrogations of the couple produced few results, but Monique soon began talking, and Michel started confessing to the murders soon thereafter. Michel made additional confessions over the years, amounting to a total of twelve victims, possibly more. Monique was given 28 years in prison while her husband received a life sentence, both without the possibility of parole. Michel died in prison in May of 2021.

CHAPTER EIGHT

Gwendolyn Graham and Catherine May Wood

Gwendolyn Gail Graham and Catherine May Wood were coworkers, friends, and eventually lovers who embarked on a murderous endeavor with the idea that these deeds would strengthen their bond. In their strange understanding of love, the two women felt that the secret of their misdeeds would serve as an oath of sorts that would bring them closer together and keep them together forever.

Just like child killers, Gwendolyn and Catherine chose weak and mostly defenseless targets when they decided to kill the elderly. Of course, the availability of such victims was a deciding factor, as both women worked as nursing assistants at the Alpine Manor nursing home in Walker, Michigan, a suburb of Grand Rapids. To make this bizarre sacrificial offering at the altar of their infatuation, Gwendolyn and Catherine murdered a total of five elderly women, usually by smothering them. The playful manner in which the pair engaged in certain aspects of their crimes and the alleged taking of souvenirs by Gwendolyn clearly showed that the two killers had undoubtedly derived pleasure from the murders. The subtle nature of the killings and the short period in which they occurred would have possibly enabled the murderers to fly under the radar had the oath of secrecy been upheld.

Turbulent Backgrounds

Gwendolyn, called Gwen by most people, was born as Gwendolyn Gail Graham on August 6 of 1963, in California, but she would spend much of her childhood living on a farm not far from the Texan city of Tyler in Smith County. This was where her family moved roughly around the time when Gwen finished fifth grade. From Gwen's early age, her father had some fairly hardline ideas on what children should learn and how they should grow up as strong individuals. His upbringing of Gwen put a lot of emphasis on matters of life, death, and hardship. For instance, Gwen was expected to watch the slaughter of chickens and pigs that were being harvested for food at the farm so that she would know where the food comes from and how.

While the harvesting of farm animals is something that plays a part in the lives of many children living in the country and isn't necessarily traumatizing if approached correctly, this wasn't where the harsh lessons for Gwen stopped. When she was a teenage girl, Gwen had a dog that she loved dearly. On one particular day, the dog got in trouble when he barked at a man passing by on horseback, spooking the horse and leading to an accident. When Gwen came home, she found that her brother had put the dog down with a gun. Gwen recalled this as a very traumatic experience, and it was when she started to behave somewhat strangely. A short while after the dog was buried, Gwen returned and dug her pet up, taking the dog's skull and teeth to keep.

Gwen was simply unable to process her emotions and move on from the loss. While she might have struggled a bit more than the average child, it's certainly not out of the ordinary for a child to have difficulty dealing with the finality of death when it's a loved one or a pet that has died. Putting aside the cruelty of the punishment inflicted on her dog just for barking, this was certainly a moment when Gwen's parents should have talked to her about death in a more positive light to try and help her through this difficult time.

However, this wasn't in line with her dad's philosophy of parenting. Throughout her childhood, Gwen also had a very weak relationship with her mother, largely due to her father's tyrannical rules around the house. When she got a bit older, and the parents separated, Gwen started to split her time between her mom and dad, so she was free to somewhat develop her relationship with her mom, but at that point, she had missed out on some necessary basics of motherly love that we all need in our formative years. In that crucial period, Gwen was barely even held or caressed, least of all by her mom.

Tenderness and love gave way to cruelty and her father's constant efforts to purposely terrorize the child with the harsh realities of life in a misguided attempt to make Gwen strong. In the end, Gwen didn't receive any nurture from either of her parents, which was probably one of the main reasons she had difficulty coping with her feelings. In effect, her father created the exact opposite effect to the one he wanted. As she got older in her teens, Gwen started to indulge in self-harm, such as cutting herself with razors and putting out cigarettes on her skin. Eventually, she accumulated dozens of scars, mostly on her arms, by the time she left home.

Gwen's eventual soulmate and partner in crime was born Catherine May Wood on March 7 of 1962. She was born on a US Air Force base close to Salt Lake, Washington because her father was a military man stationed there at that time. Cathy's parents later had another daughter, Barbara, and the family then relocated to Massachusetts. This was around the time when the US began to escalate its involvement in the

Vietnam War, and Cathy's father was soon called up to serve, which led to a period of no contact

between him and his daughters. Still, Cathy had the rest of the family, particularly her sister, with whom she was very close.

However, Cathy's social life left a lot to be desired outside of the home. She struggled to connect with other kids and form friendships, and she was also bullied. She had always been a clever young lady, and her intelligence, combined with the challenges she had experienced with other children, had led her to become something of a bookworm. She preferred to stay in to read and study, generally avoiding socialization and indulging in what her sister thought was escapism. Cathy also struggled with her weight, which, combined with the absence of her father, caused her to have low self-esteem. Even when her career-oriented father was present, he wasn't the most supportive father figure.

Despite all these problems, Cathy eventually found a boyfriend by the name of David. They went out, saw movies, hung out, and had a regular teenage relationship until Cathy went to her boyfriend's home one day to look for him. There, she met David's mother, who was very surprised to hear her asking for a "David" since she only had a daughter, which she proved by showing her photos of this girl. The girl in the picture, with long hair and a dress, was David. This was a bizarre revelation for Cathy in a decisive period of her life when she was maturing and just discovering her sexuality. It left a lasting impact on her life, not just regarding sexuality but also trust and intimacy. This was something that Cathy couldn't discuss with her parents since conversations about sexuality and dating weren't allowed.

Coworkers, Lovers, Killers

Cathy continued to date "David" despite the deception for a while, but when she was 16, she found a boyfriend who was a biological male. His name was Ken Wood, and their meeting was an important milestone in Cathy's life. This relationship got off to an unusual start right from the first date. She went to Ken's apartment after the date, but all Cathy wanted to see was proof that he was a biological male, after which she told him to get dressed. They continued dating from that point on, and it wasn't long before Cathy got pregnant, after which they moved to Michigan and had their daughter. Unfortunately, they experienced problems in their relationship after a while, most of which were related to their sex life, which Cathy felt was completely pointless. They ultimately divorced in 1986, and Cathy didn't protest her husband taking custody of the child.

After the separation, Cathy was forced to look for a job, which she searched for all over. This was how she ended up getting a job as a nurse assistant at the Alpine

Manor nursing home. The job afforded Cathy a level of independence that she had never experienced before, and she was soon standing firmly on her own two feet. After a short while on the job, Cathy met Gwen. It was a life-altering coincidence that there were quite a few lesbians employed at the nursing home, which even afforded this established reputation. Cathy was using her newfound independence to rediscover herself at the time, and the environment at her new job really fed into her unexplored sexual conundrum.

When Gwen joined the team in 1986, Cathy had already worked at the nursing home and had progressed to a minor supervisory position. Gwen and Cathy met because Cathy was Gwen's supervisor. They hit it off right away and became fast friends both at work and outside of it. Things progressed, and the two became lesbian lovers soon after. Cathy developed a strong taste for the lesbian lifestyle at this time, finding the motivation to lose weight and beginning to frequent gay bars and date numerous women. It was only with Gwen that the relationship was based on love, though.

It didn't take long for some of Gwen's darker desires and ideas to start coming out. It began with a few kinks, such as tying Cathy down during sex, choking her, or smothering her with a pillow to the edge of consciousness. Cathy didn't complain, and she indulged in this behavior as she felt it was making Gwen happy. Gwen started to talk about murdering someone as well, which Cathy initially didn't take very seriously. In time, Gwen managed to instill the idea in Cathy's mind that pain and pleasure might be intimately connected.

By January of 1987, the idea of starting to kill people had become much more serious and real. This was when the couple would begin their series of subtle killings at the Alpine Manor, which lasted for around three months. The initial idea that came from Gwen was something she called the murder game, which failed when Gwen and Cathy both realized that killing someone – even an elderly resident of a nursing home – was more difficult than they had anticipated. It wasn't for the lack of opportunity that the plan failed but for the struggle that the would-be victims put up. Nonetheless, these were old folks, some of the demented, and Gwen and Cathy remained under the radar despite having to let their victims live.

Officially, both Gwen and Cathy were held in high regard as exemplary employees by their supervisors, and, what's more, they were generally well-liked by the patients in the home. These factors likely prolonged the time it took for them to be apprehended. The killings started when Gwen and Cathy adjusted their target group, focusing only on the weakest patients who were either weak from illness or about to die. Generally, the MO was for Gwen to carry out the murder while Cathy stood at the door, observing both the murder and the hallway. Gwen usually suffocated her victims by covering their mouth and nose with a washcloth.

Gwen and Cathy would derive immense pleasure and sexual arousal from the killing every time. They would go to a storage room or another secluded area to have sex while reminiscing about the crime they had just committed minutes before. They would also occasionally collect souvenirs from their victims, including things like dentures. It wasn't just the act of killing itself that excited the couple but also the danger and potential of getting caught.

The Saga's End

The game that they initially played before deciding to opt for the weakest patients entailed the use of the patients' first-name initials to select the victims in an order that would spell out the word murder. They continued trying to find suitable names for a while, but ultimately, they had to give up this particular aspect of the game.

During their killing spree, Gwen and Cathy sometimes made jokes about killing patients in front of their coworkers, which were always laughed at and dismissed. Many of their coworkers eventually shunned the couple, partly because of their general demeanor, but also because of their proclivity for nefarious pranks. They would, for example, cause issues with their coworkers' marriages by making insinuations and sowing discord with prank calls and the like. They also liked to play with patients in various ways, such as by reshuffling them between different rooms and creating chaos for the staff. This wasn't just annoying but also potentially dangerous since patients could miss out on assistance in cases of emergency as the staff scrambled to figure out who is where.

Little did the staff know, Gwen's and Cathy's games were darker and more sinister than they could ever imagine. In addition to the twisted jokes they told in passing, some of their coworkers discovered their trophies at their place. These clues went unnoticed, whether because they didn't recognize the items or because they simply didn't care. As a result, Gwen and Cathy remained undetected for a total of five murders.

Things came to a head in April of 1987, when Cathy began to be hesitant to participate in any more killings as Gwen's bloodlust grew worse. Cathy's refusal to personally murder people as a show of devotion to Gwen gradually began to drive a wedge between them. After a change of schedule at work, Cathy was given a different shift, and she and Gwen wouldn't get to spend as much time together at work. The two grew further apart, and Gwen soon started seeing another woman, Heather Barager, more and more frequently until the two went to Texas, leaving Cathy behind.

Alone and abandoned, Cathy started to feel the weight of her conscience like never before. She struggled with this for a while until August, when she finally told her ex-husband about the things that she and Gwen had done. Ken Wood was shaken by what he heard, but he didn't know what exactly he wanted to do with these revelations, waiting more than a year before he finally decided that he should talk to the police in Grand Rapids.

Meanwhile, Gwen had been working in her hometown of Tyler, Texas, at the Mother Frances Hospital. She and Cathy remained in touch over the phone, but they didn't have much contact outside of the occasional conversation. When Ken told the police the story, they were initially reluctant to believe him and act on it. When they looked at the records of the Alpine Manor nursing home, the investigators found that around 40 people had died in the first quarter of 1987, so they had quite a bit of work ahead of them, determining which of the deaths were suspicious.

The cops initially isolated eight cases that they deemed suspicious, of which three could be eliminated after a more thorough examination of the facts and evidence. A major problem in the case was the lack of physical and forensic evidence to implicate Gwen and Cathy, but the police had testimonies to build on. Apart from Ken's testimony, the investigators were also able to obtain statements from employees at the nursing home, saying that they were having suspicions about the two girls.

The police spent some time building a case, and then they finally arrested both Gwen and Cathy in December of 1988. Gwen had already been fired from her hospital job because of the horrifying rumors that had started to circulate at the time. Despite a few sneaking suspicions that had existed, the revelations and the arrests would completely shock the vast majority of people at Alpine Manor. The news was particularly hard to swallow for those coworkers who had ignored all the dark jokes and the souvenir items that they saw in Gwen's and Cathy's possession.

Four coworkers ended up giving valuable testimonies during the trial, but Cathy's testimony was the prosecution's most important highlight. Because of her plea deal, Cathy was able to ensure that she would only be charged with second-degree murder, thus getting a sentence of 20 to 40 years. The love pact between the two girls was no more, and Cathy even testified about Gwen's attempted murders, talking about five in total, on top of the five successful killings. The jury ultimately saw through Cathy's attempts to turn the story around and portray Gwen as a scapegoat for her jealous, vindictive, and deceptive girlfriend. In early November of 1989, Gwen was given six life sentences without the possibility of parole.

CHAPTER NINE

Alton Coleman and
Debra Brown

The horrific murders that Alton Coleman committed with his accomplice, Debra Brown, were a gruesome, bloody culmination of a history of violence and sexual assault. Before meeting Debra Brown, Alton was a serial rapist and molester who had already been charged with sex crimes on several occasions between 1973 and 1983. Debra, unlike Alton, had a clean record and no criminal history. Unfortunately, she was simple, owing to a head injury that she had suffered in childhood. In addition to that, Debra was diagnosed with dependent personality disorder, making her very impressionable and prone to extreme attachment.

Although Alton was undoubtedly the mastermind and main instigator of the killings, Debra was more than willing to participate. She assisted Alton in manipulating, kidnapping, raping, savagely beating, and killing several children and adults. The prospect of legal repercussions for his previous crimes was one of the factors that drove Alton into this spree of violence. His range of mental health problems also played their part, particularly his obsession with sexual domination and control over others, which led him to target people of different backgrounds and ages, including young men.

From Victim to Monster

Alton Coleman was born on November 6 of 1955, in the town of Waukegan, to the north of Chicago. He was the third of five children. Alton's childhood was a miserable experience from the start, as he was mercilessly bullied by other children. In his youth, he would frequently wet himself, which often happened in public and at school, making him the object of constant taunts. The other kids eventually gave him the nickname of "Pissy." As a result, Alton withdrew into himself and refused to interact with other children, which was especially noticeable during his teenage years. He was also the kind of boy who kept his emotions bottled up and hidden from the world.

Given Alton's horrible home situation, his academic difficulties were unsurprising. His mother, a prostitute who had to work multiple jobs to support herself and her children, was also prone to substance abuse. When Alton was an infant, his mother reportedly threw him into a dumpster, from where he was saved by his grandmother, who took him back home. His mother would also occasionally have sex with her customers while Alton was present. Alton would usually live with his grandmother in childhood, but she was no saint either. A minister by the name of Robert Evans later testified that Alton's home environment was marked by sexual abuse in addition to other terrible things. His grandmother might have been involved in voodoo practices, which she forced Alton to participate in with things like animal sacrifice and even bestiality.

It should come as no surprise that Alton began to develop some peculiar sexual proclivities in this teens. He soon earned a reputation for being bisexual and highly sexually active, engaging in sexual acts with whomever and wherever he could. It wasn't long until Alton began to crave perverted and extreme ways of achieving sexual satisfaction. His growing sexual derangement would be one of the hallmarks of his eventual crimes.

Alton had his first run-in with the law during his teens for petty vandalism in Waukegan. While these offenses marked him as a problematic teen, he was still considered only a petty delinquent. In middle school, Alton would drop out of his education, which undoubtedly cemented his path into crime. His violent tendencies and strong sexual appetites soon led him on a path of sexual assault, starting around 1973. He would eventually become a serial rapist well known to local police, most likely starting when he and an accomplice kidnapped and raped an elderly woman in 1973, after which they also robbed her. The woman wouldn't testify to help convict Alton of rape, but he ended up doing two years in prison for robbery. In total, Coleman was charged for sex crimes six times by 1983.

In time, Alton became quite adept at putting on a façade of decency and fooling juries, which came in handy during his many arrests. This was how he was able to beat some rape charges, much to the dismay of prosecutors. In addition to that, Alton relied on supposed supernatural powers and deities to help him fight the law, including a voodoo god called Baron Samedi. When his manipulations or religion didn't work, Alton was also no stranger to witness intimidation.

Of the six charges in his ten-year rape spree, Alton managed to have two thrown out while, for others, he often managed to get plea deals and reduce his charges, which he successfully did on two occasions. He was also acquitted two times. Even though he had managed to evade serious prison time despite being a serial rapist, he had undoubtedly earned a reputation and was well-known to police throughout Illinois.

Alton was close to serious trouble in 1983 when his sister reported him for the attempted rape of her eight-year-old daughter. He was arrested and was about to be charged, but three weeks later, Alton's sister went back on her testimony and changed the story, saying that it was all just a misunderstanding and that it happens to many families. The presiding judge later expressed his shock and his belief that the woman was completely terrified of Alton.

Things were about to take an even worse turn when, in 1984, Coleman was indicted for the rape of a girl near Chicago, whose mother was an acquaintance. Afraid to face this charge, Alton decided to run away and evade the law, which led to his eventual spree of rape and murder across different states with Debra Brown, his girlfriend at the time.

Debra Brown was born in 1962 in Waukegan, just like Coleman, and she was one of eleven children in her family. Her home environment and upbringing were a lot different from Alton's, and there are no records of her being abused in any way. As previously mentioned, however, she was mentally impaired and prone to manipulation. This explains how she ended up participating in the grizzliest of crimes despite having no history of violence or crime of any kind. In fact, Debra was a perfectly nice girl before meeting Alton Coleman. Even though she was engaged, she left her family and moved in with Alton, initially to assist in the care of his grandmother.

Cross-State Rampage

After learning that he would be charged with the rape of a 14-year-old girl, Alton lost all semblance of rationality. On May 31, 1984, the police began looking for him, and he was already hiding. Debra was apprehended and questioned the next day but to no avail. On June 5, Debra and Alton crossed into Indiana and rented an apartment in Gary, where they laid low for a while until June 18. This was the day when the couple's rampage officially began with the disappearance of nine-year-old Annie and seven-year-old Tamika Turks. Little did the police know, the couple had already committed their first killing in late May when they abducted another girl, nine-year-old Vernita Wheat. They abducted the girl in Wisconsin and took her back to Waukegan on May 29, after which Alton raped and strangled her. The girl's decomposing remains weren't found until June 19, not far from where Coleman lived with his grandmother. Not long after Vernita Wheat disappeared, the FBI got involved in the search, and Alton quickly became the prime suspect.

Annie and Tamika Turks were two girls who happened to be in the wrong place at the wrong time. They were out running an errand when Alton and Debra intercepted and lured them to a secluded location in the woods, where they tied them up and began to sexually abuse them. Tamika soon started crying, which infuriated Alton, at which point he savagely stomped on the girl within an inch of her life before dumping her in the woods. The couple then forced Annie into oral sex, after which Alton raped her. During the assault, the assailants heard Tamika still crying in the woods where they had left her to die, so they went back and strangled her to death with a belt. They strangled Annie with the same belt afterward, leaving her after they thought she was dead. On the day of the disappearance, Annie was found alive, although barely, by a person passing by after the attack, but Tamika was still missing.

On the following day, the couple assumed fake identities as "Phil" and "Pam," pretending they were from Boston. They met Donna Williams, a 25-year-old girl with whom they struck up a friendship. On the evening of June 19, Donna vanished after leaving her church to meet some friends, and a search began soon thereafter. The police pursued the trail and eventually found the girl's car in Detroit, with evidence that Coleman and Brown had driven it there. A couple of weeks later, the investigators found Donna's remains not far from the car.

Just five days after abducting Donna, the couple kidnapped a 28-year-old woman in Detroit by invading her property and forcing her to drive them to Ohio. The girl fought back during the drive, deliberately crashing the car and managing to get away. The murderous duo then broke into the home of an elderly couple in Dearborn Heights. Alton and Debra proceeded to brutally beat Palmer and Marge Jones, after which they robbed their house and took their car. Before leaving for Ohio, they invaded another home in Detroit on July 2, beating an elderly woman and her partner with a wrench.

By July 5, Debra and Alton made their way to Toledo, Ohio, where they made another unfortunate friend in Reverend Ernie Jackson. While they didn't kill the man, they manipulated him into giving them the address of Virginia Temple, a single mother who lived with her five kids and was a friend of Reverend Jackson. The following day, they visited Virginia and were initially cordial. Virginia invited them to have dinner with the family, and it seemed to be a normal afternoon. Virginia and her eldest daughter, ten-year-old Rochelle, were forced to go down to the basement in the early hours of July 7. Alton and Debra first savagely beat the woman and her daughter while also raping Rochelle, after which they strangled them both to death. The bodies were then hidden in a crawl space in the basement.

The assailants then robbed the house of any valuables and left. Later that day, they invaded another home, employing their usual MO on the elderly couple living there. They tied Frank and Dorothy Duvendack down, after which they beat them, robbed their home, and took their car. A couple of days later, relatives came to check on the Temple family because Virginia wasn't returning their calls, which was when they found the remaining children all alone and traumatized. On July 11, when the investigators found the remains of Donna Williams, the FBI made Alton one of their top priorities and even placed him on their Most Wanted list.

Repercussions and Epilogue

At this point, the couple's cross-state rampage of terror was reaching its bloody culmination. On July 12, Alton and Debra came to Cincinnati and abducted 15-year-old Tonnie Storey. Witnesses reported seeing the girl the day before being led away by an African-American couple, but they thought nothing of it at that point. It was only later that a witness realized the man from the couple was Alton Coleman. Unfortunately, the girl was discovered strangled and possibly raped on July 19, though the latter could not be determined with certainty due to the state of the corpse. The murderers had left yet another trail of evidence, including forensic traces and a bracelet stolen from Virginia Temple.

The day after abducting Tonnie Storey, the couple broke into the home of Harry and Marlene Walters, a middle-aged couple. The assailants arrived at the couple's home after seeing an advertisement for the sale of their camper vehicle. This is how the murderous couple got into the house without a struggle, then they took the couple to the basement and started beating them up before robbing the place. Marlene was killed as a result of being beaten with a crowbar and other weapons.

By July 16, the marauding couple had made their way to Kentucky, where they struck up a partnership with Thomas Harris, who became their accomplice. The trio then kidnapped a 33-year-old woman by the name of Oline Carmical Junior next to a motel in Lexington. This was Alton's first attempt to kidnap someone for ransom, so they called the man's wife and demanded money. The wife agreed to exchange, but, for some reason, the kidnappers changed their minds and never came to the meeting. Instead, they put Oline in the trunk of his car and just left him in Dayton, Ohio, where he was later found.

While in Dayton, the couple came to the house of Reverend Millard Gay and his wife, Kathryn, on July 17. The Reverend had been following the news, and he soon identified Alton and Debra, but he made the mistake of telling them that about it. Alton then attacked Millard and knocked him out with a blow to the head with a pistol. Alton and Debra then tied up the couple as before and tried to strangle Kathryn, but the woman survived. After they robbed the place and were about to leave in the family's car, Alton went to shoot Kathryn to ensure she was dead, but his gun failed to discharge.

The couple then headed back to Illinois, and they sought to change their vehicle along the way in Indianapolis, which led them to murder Eugene Scott, an elderly man, for his car. They stabbed and shot him multiple times before taking his car and driving away. Alton and Debra arrived at their destination in Evanston, Illinois, and abandoned the car three days later. This was where they were finally apprehended by the authorities, ending a cross-state manhunt and a trail of destruction.

The arrest was made after the police received a valuable tip from a passing driver who recognized Alton, not because of the manhunt, but because he knew him from the old neighborhood. The killers didn't try to fight the police, and, somewhat surprisingly, they surrendered without resistance, although they tried to fool the officers by giving false names. Upon conducting a pat-down search, the arresting officers found a gun and a knife on the killers.

Alton's and Debra's attempt to present false identities didn't work, of course, and the authorities were able to quickly confirm their identities via fingerprints. Legal proceedings then ensued, and the couple would be shown no mercy by the legal system, considering the sheer scope and savagery of their crimes, which amounted to a total of eight confirmed victims. Alton chose to be his own legal counsel, perhaps hoping that he could once again work his magic on a jury, but the rampage that he had now committed was unlike anything he had ever done. Eventually, he sought to manipulate the facts and lay the blame on Debra, especially during the proceedings concerning the murder of Marlene Walters. He even had her come in as a witness, personally cross-examining her, trying to incriminate her in the process.

There was nothing Alton could do this time to evade the full extent of justice, though, and all of his attempts were abysmal failures. For the murders of Marlene Walters, Tonnie Storey, Tamika Turks, and Vernita Wheat, Alton was given four death sentences in different states. He was executed in Ohio on April 26 of 2002, at 46 years of age.

Even though she was simple and had no priors, prosecutors didn't cut Debra any slack either. For participating in the gruesome killings of Marlene Walters and Tamika Turks, the states of Ohio and Indiana both sentenced Debra to death. In 1989, however, her sentence in Ohio was reduced to life in prison by an official commutation laid down by Governor Richard Celeste. The Governor was a long-time opponent of the death penalty, but he took into account Debra's diagnosis of mental retardation. Two years later, the state of Indiana also commuted Debra's sentence to 60 years in prison, but she had also been sentenced for other convictions, so her sentences still amounted to 140 years. Remorseful Debra Brown has apologized to the families of the victims in 2005, and is still serving time in Dayton.

CHAPTER TEN

Myra Hindley and Ian Brady

The crimes perpetrated by Ian Brady and Myra Hindley, popularly known as the Moors Murderers, were yet another case of serial killers who shocked the United Kingdom. Between July 1963 and October 1965, this child-murdering couple committed their crimes in the Manchester area as well as in the city itself. The case was known as the Moor murders because the bodies of the five children that Ian and Myra killed, some of whom were raped, were buried on Saddleworth Moor, a moorland area in North West England.

The cold-blooded nature of the killings, especially Ian's remorselessness for the rest of his life, was particularly shocking. This diagnosed psychopath took pleasure in toying with the police by withholding information and preventing them from finding the bodies of some of the victims, thus robbing the tragedy-stricken families of closure. Just before he died, Brady pulled another psychopathic stunt by requesting for his ashes to be scattered on Saddleworth Moors, right at the burial grounds of his and Myra's victims. Fortunately, this request was denied by the presiding judge.

The Early Lives of Child Killers

Ian Brady was born Ian Duncan Stewart on January 2 of 1938, in Glasgow, Scotland. There weren't any indications that he experienced abuse in his home environment, but his family life was nonetheless dysfunctional in many ways. His mother, Margaret Peggy Stewart, was unmarried and working as a waitress when she gave birth to Ian. Money was always a problem, and Margaret struggled severely to provide for her boy, but there was also the matter of her child's illegitimacy since it was never determined beyond a doubt who Ian's father was.

As such, Ian would grow up without a father, at least a biological one. Margaret's story was that Ian's dad was a reporter at a particular newspaper in Glasgow and that he had died just months before Ian was born. Eventually, the pressures of 1940s single motherhood proved to be too much for Margaret, and she decided to give Ian to Mary and John Sloan, a couple who already had four children and could provide well for another.

Margaret didn't entirely abandon her son, though. She continued to work and provide what help she could while also making sure to visit Ian during his childhood. It was at a very early age when Ian first began to show various signs of problematic behavior. Initially, he was just prone to mood swings and liked to throw tantrums whenever he wouldn't get his way. Some of these tantrums could get quite extreme, such as when Ian would bang his head against the wall.

Ian was way too young to remember anything when his mother gave him to the Sloans, so he spent his first years unaware that he had been adopted. Margaret would visit, but she didn't disclose her true relation to Ian. Ian was clever, though, and, in time, he figured out the truth on his own. People in the community began to learn about Ian's background as time passed, which affected the boy who was already struggling to make friends due to his anti-social behavior, lack of interest in sports, and other issues. Ian's illegitimacy gradually became a major problem and a source of self-loathing for the boy. He became more and more withdrawing, feeling more isolated from everyone with every year that went by.

Some accounts later stated that Ian also began to torture and kill animals during his childhood, like many other serial killers, but this was something that he denied. Despite all his problems, Ian was a good student and a very bright child, on top of being handsome.

When Ian was 9, the Sloans moved to Pollok in the southwest of Glasgow. He eventually applied for and was accepted into Shawlands Academy, a secondary school known for only accepting the best students.

Unfortunately, this was also the time when Ian's behavior got worse, and he gradually lost interest in school, becoming lazy and unmotivated to excel academically. He began to engage in various delinquent activities as well, including breaking and entering, for which he was arrested twice during his teenage years. He was only 15 when he decided to completely abandon school, leaving Shawlands and instead looking for a job. He started working at a shipyard in Govan and remained on this job for around nine months, after which he sought employment with a local butcher. He even found a girlfriend during this time, one Evelyn Grant, but things didn't work out since Ian was prone to outbursts of anger and jealousy. He scared the girl off when he threatened to stab her for dancing with another boy.

Ian's run-ins with the law continued during this time, and he was eventually ordered by the court to either move back in with his mother or go to prison. His mother, who was now living in Manchester, was married to Patrick Brady. Patrick was in the business of selling fruit, so he was able to find a job for Ian, and the family began their efforts to set the boy straight. Unfortunately, it didn't take long for Ian to get back to mischief, and he eventually got in trouble for theft. He would spend the next couple of years in juvenile correctional facilities until his release in November of 1957. To the surprise of his parents, Ian started to study to improve his qualifications, eventually landing a job at a chemical distribution company called Millwards in the Manchester suburbs in 1959. Around this time, Ian began to show an interest in topics such as Nazism and the Holocaust.

Myra Hindley, Ian's eventual crime partner, was born in Manchester on July 23, 1942. Although she grew up in a close-knit family, her home environment was far from ideal, and her childhood was in many ways far worse than Ian's. Nellie and Bob, both of her parents, were physically and verbally abusive to her from an early age. Bob Hindley was also an alcoholic with a bad temper and a propensity for violence. The family was also poor, and Myra would have to move to her grandmother's place at the age of 5, after her sister, Maureen, was born in 1946.

Myra's father wasn't just ill-tempered, though. Bob was a man of violence through and through, having had significant experience with it during World War II. He taught Myra that a capacity for violence was a virtue and that she would have to stand up for herself. At age 8, Myra's dad threatened to beat her when she cried instead of retaliating after being hurt by a bully at school. After she beat the boy the next day, she was rewarded at home.

A major upset in Myra's life came in 1957 when her friend, Michael Higgins, drowned while he was swimming. He had previously invited Myra to go with him, but she had plans with another friend. Myra was a good swimmer, and when she learned of her friend's tragic end, she was devastated and guilt-ridden. Not long after this, Myra started working on her first job as a clerk in an electrical engineering company. Unlike Ian, Myra was a well-liked person who made friends everywhere she went, and her first job was no different. Myra even got engaged when she was 17, but she broke off the engagement after a change of heart.

A Joint Enterprise of Evil

A major change in Myra's life came after she got a new job at Millwards in 1961. She was only 18 at the time, but she had qualifications such as the ability to type. Myra met Ian in late July of 1961, after having been fascinated and infatuated with him for a while before that point. Much about her perception of Ian during this time came from her diary, which was thoroughly examined during the subsequent investigations. Myra's interest in Ian waned toward the end of the year, but it was reignited when Ian asked her out in December.

In time, Myra became obsessed with Ian and started to adopt many of his interests, views, and attitudes, particularly Ian's fascination with Nazism and the atrocities of Nazi Germany. During her subsequent pleas for parole in the late 1970s, Myra would make it a point to emphasize that Ian had significant sway over her. She stated that it was Ian who convinced her that there was no God and that she would have believed him even if he told her the earth was flat or the moon was made of cheese.

Myra began to change more and more, physically and otherwise, and the people in her surroundings started to take notice. Over time, Myra and Ian became more reclusive and shut off from other people, which was noticed by the people they used to hang out with. The couple focused more on reading books about philosophy and crime, becoming regulars at the local library. They also started frequenting gun ranges and learned to use weapons, with Myra trying for some time to acquire a rifle legally. After this failed, she eventually bought pistols from fellow gun club members. The couple considered a life of crime centered primarily on bank robbery for a time, but none of their plans came to fruition.

Instead, according to Myra, Ian began talking about murder in the summer of 1963, and is particularly fixated on the idea of planning and committing a perfect murder. Ian told Myra about the fascination he had with Compulsion, a 1956 novel written by Meyer Levin and later made into a movie, which revolves around two rich men who decide to kill a young boy and get away with it. That summer, Ian and Myra had already started living together at Myra's grandmother's house on Bannock Street.

On July 12 of 1963, the couple would take steps to make Ian's fantasy a reality. Their first victim was Pauline Reade, a 16-year-old girl who went to school with Myra's sister, but she wasn't Ian's first choice. They tracked down a victim by having Myra drive around in a rented van while Ian followed behind on a motorcycle. Ian took it upon himself to scout for a suitable victim and, upon finding one, he was supposed to flash his headlight to signal to Myra. He found his first potential victim on Gorton Lane, a girl who was only 8 years old. Myra realized that she knew this girl and decided not to stop for her, waiting instead for another, older victim. That's how the couple eventually stumbled upon Pauline Reade.

Ian and Myra talked Pauline into the van without force, and they asked her if she could help them search for a glove around Saddleworth Moor, and Pauline was glad to help. As with most of the murders, there are considerable differences between the accounts of the two killers. According to Myra, Ian took Pauline out onto the moor while she stayed behind in the van. Ian Brady then returned after half an hour, and the two went outside to see Pauline, who was half-naked and had her throat slashed to the point of near-decapitation. Ian allegedly replied, "Of course," when Myra asked if he had raped the girl. Ian, however, later claimed that Myra was right beside him the entire time, participating in both the murder and the rape.

Hindley and Brady would strike again on November 23 of 1963 when they picked up 12-year-old John Kilbride under the pretense of giving him a ride home from a market in Ashton-under-Lyne. The boy was out late, so the killers were able to convince him that he should get home as fast as possible, and they also used sherry to lure him in. After making a couple of detours, they told the victim, as before, that they were looking for an expensive glove on Saddleworth Moor, asking for the boy's help in the search. Myra later said that the murder went the same way as the first one, with Ian taking the victim out on the moor, raping him, and finally killing him. Ian first tried to slash the boy's throat, but when that didn't work, he strangled the victim with rope, possibly a shoelace. The authorities organized a massive search for the boy, but to no avail.

The couple's next murder was on June 16 of 1964, when they abducted 12-year-old Keith Bennett, whom they picked up in Longsight as he was walking to his grandmother's house. Myra lured the boy in by asking for his help to load some goods into her vehicle, after which she and Ian offered the boy a ride home.

Instead, they drove Keith to their old killing grounds on Saddleworth Moor and killed him in a similar manner to their previous victims.

Ian and Myra committed one more murder in 1964, this time on Boxing Day, December 26. The couple went to a funfair in Ancoat's to hunt for a new victim when they noticed a 10-year-old girl by the name of Lesley Ann Downey, who appeared to be alone at that moment. They then fooled the girl into following them to their car by pretending they needed help to carry their groceries. They didn't take their victim to the moors this time, instead, they returned to their new home on Wardle Book Avenue. They then forced the child to undress, gagged her, and initially made her pose for photos before they both raped her. Ian most likely killed the girl by strangling her with a string, as with other victims. Also, as before, Myra claimed that she wasn't present for the murder and was instead in the bathroom filling up a bath. Ian not only denied this but said that Myra personally killed the girl. After the murder, they buried Lesley on Saddleworth Moor as with the others.

Final Crimes and Arrest

After the killing of Lesley Ann Downey, Myra and Ian didn't kill again until autumn of 1965 when, on October 6, they went to the Manchester Central railway station to prowl for a new victim. Myra stayed in the car while Ian went to look for someone, returning after only a few minutes with 17-year-old Edward Evans, introducing him to Myra as Ian's sister. It's not clear how exactly the couple got Edward to follow them home to Wardle Brook Avenue, but Ian would later claim that Edward was lured in with partying and a potential sexual encounter.

This time, the couple would have an accomplice in David Smith, who was Myra's brother-in-law since August of 1964 when he married her sister, Maureen. This was a difficult marriage because Myra, and particularly the rest of her family, disliked Smith and had never approved of the marriage. David Smith was a man with a violent past who had multiple criminal offenses under his belt, including violent offenses and burglary. Unlike Myra and the rest of the Hindley's, Ian had a lot of respect for David Smith, and the two had been getting along very well since the first time they met. Myra had been growing jealous of their closeness for some time, but she was more concerned that David had learned too much about Ian and her.

Ian sent Myra to find Smith and bring him over before the murder of Edward Evans. When Smith came over, Ian initially had him waiting in the kitchen while he went to "bring the wine." According to Smith's subsequent testimony, he had been in the kitchen for about a minute when he heard horrible screams and

Myra calling him to come and help, shouting. When David walked into the room, he saw Edward on the couch and Ian standing over him, dealing a devastating blow to his head with a hatchet. After splitting the boy's skull, Ian proceeded to strangle him with a cable.

The following morning, David Smith returned to help Hindley and Brady to get Edward over to the moor and bury him. He returned home late that night, trying to process what he had participated in, perhaps in an attempt to keep the secret. However, as soon as he sat down with his wife for a cup of tea, David became nauseous and could no longer crawl out from underneath the weight of his guilt. The following morning, David went to a payphone and called the police, who soon picked him up and took his statement about the gruesome events that had transpired.

After the arrest of Ian and Myra and the gradual accumulation of evidence against them, the couple initially joined forces to try and lay the blame on David Smith. The police immediately searched their apartment and found a plethora of disturbing evidence, such as the infamous photo of Myra crouching and posing on the grave of John Kilbride. When it became clear that they couldn't shift the blame, Myra and Ian turned on each other, each attempting to negotiate a plea deal and lessen the punishment. It didn't work for either of them, and they were eventually sentenced to life in prison, probably because the death penalty had been abolished in England only a short while before their arrest. While the others were found, the body of Keith Bennett has never been located. Hindley and Brady died in prison in 2002 and 2017, respectively.

Conclusion

Most regular people tend to imagine serial killers as disturbed loners who lurk around in the shadows and hide from the world. One particularly scary thing about killer couples, apart from their foul deeds, is that they show us that murderers, although rare, are just common enough to occasionally run into each other and join forces. It's a reminder that they walk around among us, often hidden under a façade of complete normalcy to the point where they can lead regular family lives.

In marriage and other forms of relationships, these couples can even be worse than individual murderers because they can pool their resources and encourage each other. Whereas a lone serial killer may be discouraged or even afraid to continue in some cases, murderers who have found a kindred deranged soul will have a source of support, which will likely embolden them in their terrible endeavors, give them ideas, or even make them feel like they aren't doing anything wrong.

As such, the support and comfort of a relationship generally make these people worse and more dangerous. This is a great example of how something that is otherwise a good thing can become warped and completely turned around when it comes to these disturbed individuals. Perhaps the most perplexing aspect of the story is that such people are capable of falling in love. Most regular people are unable to comprehend how they can be so cruel while still showing affection for each other.

Even though these killers probably have a very different outlook on love, there is no denying that there was real devotion at work in some of these cases. The important thing to remember is that their actions were not motivated by love. It may have enabled and encouraged them, but the true seed and the root cause of their evil are most likely much older and deeper.

References

All That's Interesting. (2017, November 22). The Horrifying Story Of David Parker Ray, The "Toy Box Killer." All That's Interesting; All That's Interesting. https://allthatsinteresting.com/david-parker-ray-toy-box-killer

Alton Coleman | Murderpedia, the encyclopedia of murderers. (n.d.). Murderpedia.org. Retrieved August 3, 2021, from https://murderpedia.org/male.C/c1/coleman-alton.htm

Alton Coleman and Debra Brown. (n.d.). Criminal Minds Wiki. https://criminalminds.fandom.com/wiki/Alton_Coleman_and_Debra_Brown

Amisha Padnani. (2017, May 17). The Moors Murders: A Notorious Couple and Their Young Prey. The New York Times. https://www.nytimes.com/2017/05/17/world/europe/moors-murders-ian-brady-myra-hindley-victims.html

Anglis, J. (2021, April 26). Meet The Serial Killer Couple Who Murdered Their Way Across The Midwest In 1984. All That's Interesting. https://allthatsinteresting.com/alton-coleman

Bartlette, D. R. (2019a, February 11). The San Francisco Witch Killers. Medium. https://delanirbartlette.medium.com/the-san-francisco-witch-killers-9c8acd6e915f

Bartlette, D. R. (2019b, February 18). Gwen Graham and Cathy Wood. Medium. https://delanirbartlette.medium.com/gwen-graham-and-cathy-wood-ac774d3c7750

Blanco, J. I. (n.d.-a). Carol Bundy | Murderpedia, the encyclopedia of murderers. Murderpedia.org. https://murderpedia.org/female.B/b/bundy-carol.htm

Britain's worst serial killers haunt a city, decades after their grisly crimes. (n.d.). Www.9news.com.au. Retrieved July 19, 2021, from https://www.9news.com.au/world/serial-killers-fred-rosemary-west-haunt-a-city-decades-after-their-grisly-crimes/cdf89538-64d7-4cc2-9285-aa16c1e846e4

Campbell, J. (2021, May 5). The Toy Box Killer: How a depraved life and accomplices helped a serial killer pull off dozens of murders. Front Page Detectives. https://www.frontpagedetectives.com/p/serial-killer-new-mexico-torture-murder

Catherine May Wood | Murderpedia, the encyclopedia of murderers. (n.d.). Murderpedia. org. Retrieved August 2, 2021, from https:// murderpedia.org/female.W/w/wood-catherine.htm

David Parker Ray. (n.d.). Criminal Minds Wiki. https:// criminalminds.fandom.com/wiki/David_Parker_Ray

Debra Brown | Murderpedia, the encyclopedia of murderers. (n.d.). Murderpedia.org. https:// murderpedia.org/female.B/b/brown-debra.htm

Details About The Life And Crimes Of The San Francisco Witch Killers. (n.d.). Ranker. Retrieved July 22, 2021, from https://www.ranker.com/ list/san-francisco-witch-killers/ella-talkin

Ex-wife of France's "Ogre of the Ardennes" serial killer may face justice. (2021, May 13). RFI. https:// www.rfi.fr/en/france/20210513-ex-wife-of-france-s-ogre-of-the-ardennes-serial-killer-may-face-justice

Families denied justice as French serial killer Michel Fourniret dies at 79. (2021, May 11). RFI. https://www. rfi.fr/en/france/20210511-families-denied-justice-as-french-serial-killer-michel-fourniret-dies-at-79

Fourniret | Journeyman Pictures. (n.d.). Www. journeyman.tv. Retrieved August 2, 2021, from https:// www.journeyman.tv/film_documents/4036/transcript/

George, K. (2017, May 8). The Bizarre Case Of The California Witch Killers. Oxygen Official Site. https://www.oxygen.com/blogs/the-bizarre-case-of-the-california-witch-killers

Gwendolyn Graham | Murderpedia, the encyclopedia of murderers. (n.d.). Murderpedia.org. https://murderpedia.org/female.G/g/graham-gwendolyn.htm

Gwendolyn Graham and Cathy Wood. (n.d.). Notoriouswomen. Retrieved August 2, 2021, from https://notoriouswomen.jimdofree.com/gwendolyn-graham/

Heim, B. (2020, December 17). Who were the California witch killers? See the strangest true crime story. Film Daily. https://filmdaily.co/obsessions/true-crime/california-witch-killers/

Henry Lee Lucas. (n.d.). Criminal Minds Wiki. https://criminalminds.fandom.com/wiki/Henry_Lee_Lucas

Holley, G. (2021, January 7). The Toy Box Killer A.K.A. David Parker Ray: Serial Killer Who Sexually Tortured Women In His Trailer. History Daily. https://historydaily.org/toy-box-killer-david-parker-ray-facts-stories-trivia

Ian Brady and Myra Hindley. (n.d.). Criminal Minds Wiki. https://criminalminds.fandom.com/wiki/Ian_Brady_and_Myra_Hindley

Ishak, N. (2021, January 14). Meet The Sadistic Serial Killer Couple That Terrorized L.A.'s Sunset Strip In 1980. All That's Interesting. https://allthatsinteresting.com/doug-clark

James Clifford Carson | Murderpedia, the encyclopedia of murderers. (n.d.). Murderpedia.org. Retrieved July 21, 2021, from https://murderpedia.org/male.C/c/carson-james-clifford.htm

Joanna Parrish murder: French serial killer "confesses" to 1990 killing. (2018, February 16). BBC News. https://www.bbc.com/news/uk-england-gloucestershire-43090688

Juan Ignacio Blanco. (n.d.-b). Ian Brady | Murderpedia, the encyclopedia of murderers. Murderpedia.org. https://murderpedia.org/male.B/b/brady-ian.htm

Juan Ignacio Blanco. (n.d.-c). Myra Hindley | Murderpedia, the encyclopedia of murderers. Murderpedia.org. https://murderpedia.org/female.H/h/hindley-myra.htm

Juan Ignacio Blanco. (n.d.-d). Rosemary West | Murderpedia, the encyclopedia of murderers. Murderpedia.org. https://murderpedia.org/female.W/w/west-rosemary.htm

Juan Ignacio Blanco. (2002). David Parker Ray | Murderpedia, the encyclopedia of murderers. Murderpedia.org. http://murderpedia.org/male.R/r/ray-david-parker.htm

Juan Ignacio Blanco. (2010). Paul Bernardo | Murderpedia, the encyclopedia of murderers. Murderpedia.org. https://murderpedia.org/male.B/b/bernardo-paul.htm

Juan Ignacio Blanco. (2012). Karla Homolka | Murderpedia, the encyclopedia of murderers. Murderpedia.org. https://murderpedia.org/female.H/h/homolka-karla.htm

Juan Ignacio Blanco. (2019). Frederick West | Murderpedia, the encyclopedia of murderers. Murderpedia.org. https://murderpedia.org/male.W/w/west-frederick.htm

Juan Ignacio Blanco. (2020). Henry Lee Lucas | Murderpedia, the encyclopedia of murderers. Murderpedia.org. http://www.murderpedia.org/male.L/l/lucas-henry-lee.htm

Key events in the Bernardo/Homolka case. (2010, June 17). CBC. https://www.cbc.ca/news/canada/key-events-in-the-bernardo-homolka-case-1.933128

Lavender, J. (2020, May 12). Ian Brady's horrifying dying wish was sick final twist to punish his victims. Mirror. https://www.dailyrecord.co.uk/news/crime/ian-bradys-horrifying-dying-wish-22009121

Lease, L. (n.d.). The Heinous Crimes of Henry Lee Lucas and Otis Toole. Criminal. Retrieved July 22, 2021, from https://vocal.media/criminal/the-heinous-crimes-of-henry-lee-lucas-and-otis-toole

Margaritoff, M. (2020, August 29). When She Found Out Her Boyfriend Was A Serial Killer, She Helped Him Find New Victims. All That's Interesting. https://allthatsinteresting.com/cindy-hendy

Michel Fourniret | Murderpedia, the encyclopedia of murderers. (n.d.). Murderpedia.org. Retrieved July 31, 2021, from https://murderpedia.org/male.F/f/fourniret.htm

Michel Fourniret: Jailed French serial killer dies aged 79. (2021, May 10). BBC News. https://www.bbc.com/news/world-europe-57061856

Michel Fourniret: Ogres of the Ardennes. (n.d.). Crime+Investigation UK. Retrieved August 2, 2021, from https://www.crimeandinvestigation.co.uk/crime-files/michel-fourniret

Murderous Nursing Home Aides Guilty Of Killing Multiple Patients In Michigan. (2020, September 26). Oxygen Official Site. https://www.oxygen.com/license-to-kill/crime-news/cathy-wood-gwendolyn-graham-guilty-nursing-home-murders

Muro, M. (2020, June 29). How "Toy Box Killer" David Parker Ray Enslaved Women In His Torture Chamber With Help From His Girlfriend. Oxygen Official Site. https://www.oxygen.com/killer-couples/crime-news/how-toy-box-killer-david-parker-ray-and-cindy-hendy-tortured-women

Oliver, M. (2018, May 20). Henry Lucas And Ottis Toole Became Lovers And Then Murdered Their Way Across The United States. All That's Interesting. https://allthatsinteresting.com/henry-lee-lucas-ottis-toole

Ottis Toole. (2014, April 2). Biography. https://www.biography.com/crime-figure/ottis-toole

Ottis Toole | Murderpedia, the encyclopedia of murderers. (n.d.). Murderpedia.org. https://murderpedia.org/male.T/t/toole-ottis.htm

Paul Bernardo and Karla Homolka. (2019). Criminal Minds Wiki. https://criminalminds.fandom.com/wiki/Paul_Bernardo_and_Karla_Homolka

Paul Bernardo and Karla Homolka Case | The Canadian Encyclopedia. (2018). Thecanadianencyclopedia.ca. https://www.thecanadianencyclopedia.ca/en/article/paul-bernardo-and-karla-homolka-case

Paul, readNovember 17, erson T. C. E. min, & comments)`; }); });, 2014-10:20AM/* global newscorpau */ fetch then then innerHTML = `${data} comments`; document querySelector innerHTML += ` . (2014, November 16). Virgin hunter's "bloody muse" lured his victims. Heraldsun. https://www.heraldsun.com.au/news/law-order/true-crime-scene/michel-fourniret-french-serial-killer-craved-only-virgins-to-rape-and-murder/news-story/07e873fd5b64f10f14a7af83be43fc9d

Reporter, J. C., Staff. (n.d.). Recounting the Bernardo trial. Battlefords News-Optimist. Retrieved July 21, 2021, from https://www.newsoptimist.ca/features/first-person/recounting-the-bernardo-trial-1.24169440

Stuart, G. (2020, October 9). Forty Years Ago, the Sunset Strip Killers Terrorized L.A. Los Angeles Magazine. https://www.lamag.com/citythinkblog/sunset-strip-killers/

Suspect's Daughter Is Arrested in Sex And Torture Case. (1999, April 27). The New York Times. https://www.nytimes.com/1999/04/27/us/suspect-s-daughter-is-arrested-in-sex-and-torture-case.html

The 12 victims of Fred and Rosemary West. (2021, May 27). BBC News. https://www.bbc.com/news/uk-england-gloucestershire-57182844

The Horrifying Case of the Sunset Strip Killers. (2018). The Lineup; Open Road Media. https://the-line-up.com/sunset-strip-killers

The Ogre Of The Ardennes: The Sadistic Crimes Of Michel Fourniret. (n.d.). Ranker. Retrieved August 2, 2021, from https://www.ranker.com/list/facts-about-michel-fourniret-the-ogre-of-the-ardenne/cat-mcauliffe

The Socians. (2020, June 20). Susan & James Carson: Bizzare Story of a Witch Serial Killer Couple who Planned

to Kill President. Socians; Socians. https://www.thesocians.
com/post/susan-james-carson-bizzare-story-of-a-witch-
serial-killer-couple-who-planned-to-kill-president

Tron, G. (2018, March 1). Was Carol Bundy A
Victim Or The Mastermind Behind The "Sunset
Strip Killers"? Oxygen Official Site. https://www.
oxygen.com/mysteries-scandals/crime-time/
carol-bundy-victim-mastermind-sunset-strip-killers

writer, C. M. P. I. C. M. is a, Enforcement, F. L. P. D. W.
W. with L., Crime, I. F. I., & Montaldo, fraud our editorial
process C. (n.d.). Female Serial Killer Debra Brown
Started Her Murder Spree at Age 21. ThoughtCo. https://
www.thoughtco.com/serial-killer-debra-brown-973117

Writer, J. C. (2018, April 17). My Struggle To Find Peace
As The Daughter Of A Serial Killer. HuffPost. https://
www.huffpost.com/entry/jenn-carson-serial-killer-fat
her_n_5ad4f388e4b0edca2cbcc29a

Wynne, K. (2019, December 6). Everything you need to
know about "The Confession Killer" friendship between
Ottis Toole and Henry Lee Lucas. Newsweek. https://
www.newsweek.com/true-story-confession-killer-
henry-lee-lucas-serial-killer-ottis-toole-1475957

Printed in Great Britain
by Amazon

79803042R00088